LOOKING FOR
AN ENEMY

LOOKING FOR AN ENEMY

8 ESSAYS ON ANTISEMITISM

Edited by **JO GLANVILLE**

W. W. NORTON & COMPANY
Independent Publishers Since 1923

First published in the United Kingdom by Short Books UK.
First American Edition 2022

ISBN 978-1-324-02065-3

W. W. Norton & Company, Inc., 500 Fifth Avenue, New York, N.Y. 10110
www.wwnorton.com

W. W. Norton & Company Ltd., 15 Carlisle Street, London W1D 3BS

1 2 3 4 5 6 7 8 9 0

CONTENTS

INTRODUCTION

Jo Glanville

ANTISEMITISM NEVER GOES out of fashion. It adapts endlessly to the anxieties of the age. Pandemic? Jews are behind it. Immigration? Jews are orchestrating it. Terrorist atrocity? A Zionist plot. Over the past few years these Jewish conspiracy theories have entered the mainstream, from President Trump's rumour-mongering about Jewish investor and philanthropist George Soros's supposed malign influence to Labour Party members in the UK accusing Jews of various Zionist plots. In Europe and America, antisemitic incidents have reached an historic high. In 2018, the German government appointed its first antisemitism commissioner; in 2020, the United Nations announced a special envoy to combat antisemitism. The evidence adds up to a startling trend: more than 75 years after the Holocaust, despite education programmes and international memorialisation of the genocide, antisemitism is circulating across the political spectrum.

For this anthology, I asked writers in Europe, Israel and America to contribute essays that would offer a greater understanding of antisemitism's resurgence, reporting from their home fronts as well as taking on the universal themes. Some essays include illuminating and moving memoir, others political or historical commentary. They are a reminder that the far right remains a bigger threat to Jews than the left, that the roots of contemporary antisemitism run deep and long pre-date the Holocaust and the foundation of Israel, and that each country has its own complex relationship with Jews, shaping an often inadequate response to antisemitism. All bring insight into antisemitism's enduring appeal and the factors that enable it to survive. In the title essay, Daniel Trilling shows how the Jewish conspiracy theory is the glue that binds disparate far right groups together. Modern antisemitism is not, he argues, a continuation of an ancient prejudice, but the search for an enemy to blame in turbulent times. In France, as Natasha Lehrer reveals, Jews paradoxically find themselves sidelined from the current debate on racism, even though they are still frequent targets of antisemitism. In Poland, where discussion of Polish participation in the Holocaust has been outlawed, Mikołaj Grynberg describes a childhood overshadowed by the impact of antisemitism on his family. As an adult, he is encountering the same open racism that his grandparents faced.

All racism shares the idea that the minority group will inflict some kind of harm on the majority, but antisemitism is underpinned by a belief that Jews are secretly in control and intend to use their power to ill effect, whether to control the media or global finance. The idea that Jews are plotting harm has been repeated so often that it has come to be treated as fact – whether the respected actor Maxine Peake stating in an interview in 2020 that Israeli secret services trained the US police in the tactics that killed African-American George Floyd (for which she apologised) or the much repeated claim regarding the Rothschild family's global control. In her book *Denying the Holocaust* (which famously resulted in Holocaust denier David Irving's failed libel suit), Deborah Lipstadt showed how the transformation of Jews from victims into victimisers is central to Holocaust denial: deniers accuse Jews of creating a myth of genocide in order to extort reparations from Germany and fund Israel, as part of a Zionist masterplan. It is a chilling inversion of victimhood that characterises most antisemitism.

This is a narrative that has cemented prejudice and reaffirms a deeply entrenched cultural belief that goes back to the origins of Christianity. The vilification of Jews as sinful betrayers, killers of Christ, is so fundamentally rooted in Christian culture that it may explain why, even in a secular society, there is still a sense that it's actually reasonable not to like Jews. It has been culturally acceptable to dislike Jews for far longer than it has been taboo to discriminate against them. In his revelatory book

Anti-Judaism, the historian David Nirenberg has shown how hostility towards Judaism, and Jews, was transmitted from early Christianity into western philosophy – it is embedded in the very DNA of western culture.

In the UK, the re-emergence of antisemitism is a shock, partly because we still think of ourselves as the good guys: we defeated Hitler, we're on the side of the Jews. However, as the historian Tony Kushner has shown, antisemitism continued in Britain throughout the war, and afterwards. "The Jewish problem is created by the Jews themselves," Kushner quotes from the July 1946 Mass Observation social survey, which captured the views of members of the public. "Nobody would interfere with Jews, not even Nazis, if they had not made themselves so conspicuous and hateful. The best solution would be for the Jews to pipe down."

So antisemitism has never gone away, not even in the face of the genocide of European Jews. What's new is an unashamed, though sometimes veiled, antisemitism in political discourse, alongside the rise in antisemitic hate crimes. Some commentators have put this visibility down to the rise of populist politics, on left and right, which has long been a feature of modern antisemitism, playing on the notion of an exploitative elite and echoing conspiracy theories. Others have observed the transition of far-right views into the mainstream, as Daniel Trilling investigates in his essay. Nor can antisemitism be separated from a rising xenophobia that targets Muslims and migrants, and which has also been encouraged by politicians, including

President Trump and various European leaders. Some observers have claimed credibly that anti-migrant rhetoric influenced Robert Bowers' assault on worshippers at the Tree of Life synagogue in Pittsburgh on 27 October 2018, the worst attack on Jews in US history. Bowers accused Jews of bringing "evil" Muslims into the US.

Although Muslims and Jews clearly share a common enemy (and have historically been cast as co-conspirators), extremist European Muslims have emerged as a more recent threat to Jews. In an EU survey in 2018, respondents were asked to describe the perpetrator of the most serious incident of antisemitic harassment experienced in the past five years. Respondents in 30 per cent of cases identified the perpetrator as "someone with Muslim extremist views", while 13 per cent identified the perpetrator as "someone with a right-wing political view". Natasha Lehrer details some of the most shocking incidents in France over the past decade in her essay, including the murder of Jewish hostages at the Hypercacher kosher supermarket in 2015. However, novelist Olga Grjasnowa challenges the current narrative in Germany that singles out Muslims as the greatest threat to German Jews, when in fact the majority of antisemitic crimes in 2019 were committed by the far right, a trend that continued in 2020.

Despite the clear rise in antisemitism, there is a perplexing failure to recognise it. It's quite possible to be an avowed anti-racist and still be an antisemite, as members of the Labour Party under Jeremy Corbyn demonstrated.

How is that feasible? European and American Jews do not fit with the model of victims of racism: they are perceived as privileged and as white, and therefore cannot be oppressed. As Philip Spencer observes in his essay on antisemitism and the left, they are seen as part of the global power structure. This resistance to viewing Jews as casualties of racism is part of the long history of seeing them as oppressors themselves, the victims as victimisers. The response of Jeremy Corbyn and his supporters in the UK to the Equality and Human Rights Commission's damning report on antisemitism in the Labour Party in October 2020 replayed this distorted narrative: the scale of the problem was "dramatically overstated for political reasons", Corbyn claimed, by the media and by opponents. After his suspension from the Labour Party, it was Corbyn who was identified as the victim by his supporters, while Jews were apparently exaggerating their victimhood or even (once again) behind a conspiracy. It is deeply disturbing that Corbyn and his supporters continued to cast doubt on the spread of antisemitism in the party after a statutory public body identified a culture that not only failed to do enough to prevent racism against Jews but even accepted it.

This perception of Jews as victimisers has most perniciously been transposed to Israel: when the Israeli state discriminates against Palestinians and violates their rights, here are the Jews as a people being oppressors once again (now characterised, on the left, as colonialist oppressors). As Philip Spencer comments in his essay, it is another instance of "Jews behaving badly". It was European antisemitism that made Zionism as a movement necessary: a Jewish state was a political solution to persecution. So it is perhaps not surprising, though it's always shocking, when Europeans reach for the antisemitic arsenal (which has since gone global) to denounce Israel. This plays out in the repeated use of old antisemitic tropes to attack Israel, including cartoons of bloodthirsty Israeli soldiers who look like caricatures of Jews from Nazi propaganda.

Yet it is a mistake to claim that anti-Zionism is always equivalent to antisemitism, as a number of leading Jewish figures in the UK did at the height of the antisemitism row in the Labour Party. As Israeli historian Tom Segev points out in his essay for this anthology, not all Jews are Zionists and a negative attitude towards Israel or Zionist ideology should not be regarded automatically as a display of antisemitism. There is continuing confusion about the line between antisemitism and anti-Zionism, and the recent widespread adoption of the International Holocaust Remembrace Alliance (IHRA) definition of antisemitism has not turned out to be a satisfactory solution, while it has polarised opinion. Although it is now widely accepted as an international benchmark, a number of leading commentators and lawyers have pointed out its lack of clarity. In 2016, the UK Parliament's Home Affairs Select Committee called for clarifications to protect open discussion of Israel and Palestine.

Seven of the 11 examples illustrating the definition

relate to Israel, including: "Applying double standards by requiring of [Israel] a behaviour not expected or demanded of any other democratic nation". Yet Israel is not like "any other democratic nation": it is an ethnic state that has occupied territory in breach of international law for more than 50 years. As the writer and former UK appeal court judge Stephen Sedley has pointed out, the IHRA's formulation puts the uniqueness of the occupation beyond criticism. In October 2020, Gavin Williamson, the UK government's education secretary, threatened funding cuts if universities failed to adopt the definition, although it is not legally binding. Yet in the US, even a lead drafter of the definition, Kenneth Stern, has criticised the chill on political speech on campus. As Rabbi Jill Jacobs details in her essay, Trump's Executive Order on Combating Antisemitism in 2019 (which adopted the IHRA definition) constrains free speech when it comes to criticising Israel: support for right-wing Israeli policy, Jacobs observes, has become equated with support for Jews. At a time when antisemitism is on the rise and the prospects of a two-state solution have rapidly diminished, a non-partisan definition is more urgent than ever. Philip Spencer offers a different view of the definition in this anthology, criticising the response of the Labour Party's National Executive Committee as opposing the very existence of an Israeli state.

Antisemitism is a political football, and this will always make it particularly treacherous to referee any debate about its meaning or disputes about its occurrence. The very word is a political creation, popularised in the late 19th century by Wilhelm Marr, a German antisemite, that rebranded hatred of Jews in racial, rather than religious terms, as antisemitism was emerging as a political movement. So it has always been a loaded term – questionable in its literal meaning ("semitic" is a linguistic term that applies to a group of languages including Arabic as well as Hebrew) and often deployed not simply to call out racism but for political advantage – by Jews against Jews, as well as non-Jews. When the Jewish-American writer Peter Beinart wrote an article in July 2020 advocating a one-state solution for Israel and Palestine, with equal rights for Israelis and Palestinians, Jewish critics branded him an antisemite. The State Department's threat to denounce Amnesty International, Human Rights Watch and Oxfam as antisemitic in autumn 2020 is one of the most egregious instances of wilfully abusing the term to undermine critics (and another example of Jill Jacobs's argument that the aim is in fact to support Israeli policy, not to defend Jews – all these organisations have documented Israeli human rights abuse). Anyone who makes the accusation of antisemitism in a public forum is aware of its power to shock and silence. As Tom Segev points out in his essay on the use and abuse of the Holocaust, Israeli political leaders have routinely discredited their rivals by comparing each other to Hitler.

So this is a subject that is fraught with difficulty, from making sense of the growing hostility towards Jews that has resulted in fatalities in Europe and the US, to the arguments about the meaning of antisemitism and the sometimes cynical misuse of the term. This anthology provides some navigation and perhaps a deeper under-standing not only of the contemporary face of antisemi-tism, but the long history that has informed its continuity.

LOOKING FOR
AN ENEMY

FAMILY STORIES

Mikołaj Grynberg

Translated by Sean Gasper Bye

"GRYNBERG, WHAT KIND of a name is that?"

"Jewish."

"Oh, I'm really sorry. 'Scuse me for asking, does that mean that you're...?"

"A Jew."

"From your parents?"

"Well exactly, from my parents."

"Your mum and your dad both?"

"My mum and my dad both."

"We're really sorry this is how it's turned out, but we don't want to have anything to do with you."

I was working on a series of photographs about vanishing professions. I'd come across an industrial mangle in Warsaw's Szmulki district, which before the war had been a Jewish area. A pair of 50-year-olds in white aprons greeted me. They were nice, but when the time came to sign a release to use their images, they noticed my last name on the form and the spell was broken.

History had given them an ex-Jewish home, along with the comfort of not knowing the fate of its previous owners.

After the war, Poland became a country stripped of its history. Years of communist education saw to it that the Holocaust did not appear in textbooks. A crude narrative was enforced: the Germans attacked Poland, which bore heavy losses, but thanks to the fraternal aid of the Soviet Union the country was liberated. In school they didn't teach us about the Holocaust or the ghettos. As for Auschwitz, we knew it was a death camp where over a million people were murdered. Unmentioned in the official history curriculum was the fact that the majority of them were Jews.

That was something I learned at family gatherings on Sundays and holidays.

I was born to a family of Holocaust survivors. Auschwitz, numbers tattooed on forearms, ghettos and hiding spots on the Aryan side formed the main course of our dinners.

For a long time, I thought that everyone had to go to a camp, that such was the order of things. I treated my grandparents' stories like a peculiar kind of instruction. I mentally prepared myself for sleeping in bitter cold on three-level bunks in Birkenau. I wondered what it was like to go to the latrine with everyone else from my block. I didn't know if I could deal with the kapo – a prisoner put in charge of fellow inmates by the SS. I knew there were occasionally gentler ones, the kind who only beat you when a German was watching, but I didn't know how to make sure I ended up with one of those. I considered very seriously whether I'd rather have a number tattooed on the inside or outside of my arm. I didn't know if I'd be able to maintain as much dignity as my grandmother had, when some ethnic Poles made me watch them unpacking parcels of food from their loved ones. There was no question that, as a Jew, no such surprise gifts would be coming for me. I was sure that just as they had with my grandma, they'd make me stand across from them and watch them eat the bread and marmalade they'd been sent.

"Why did you have to watch them eat?" I asked my grandma 30 years after the liberation of the camp.

"I guess they wanted to feel like they weren't the worst, that there were other people who were worse off than them."

"You couldn't say no?"

"I could have, but they'd have beaten me to death."

"And I wouldn't have been born."

"Maybe you would have, since I'd already had your mum."

"Was she with you in the camp?" I asked.

That was the first time I heard my mum's story. She wasn't in the camp; fate cast her from one orphanage to another, and finally to a few other places – in France as well as Poland.

"Why was mum in France and you were in Poland?"

3

"They deported both grandpa and me from Paris, but your mum was lucky and she stayed there."

"How old was she?"

"Three."

"Why did this happen in France?"

"We wanted to go to university, and in Poland they wouldn't allow us to. I went to France and graduated there, I met your grandpa and I had your mum."

"You didn't get into university here?"

"I did, but they didn't take me. They called it numerus clausus; there was a very limited number of spaces for Jews. And if you did get in, they told you to sit in separate seats or stand, while the Polish students would get to sit comfortably. Antisemitic gangs would break into the college and beat people bloody."

Of my four grandparents, three went to university, all of them abroad.

A long time went by before I believed there were no longer any camps in Poland. What a relief! The world filled with colour. Until then I'd been immensely anxious that I wouldn't get a degree and might lose my family. Though the topic had never been far from my mind, I still hadn't known what I'd do to survive.

I gained some mental distance, and apparently became a much cheerier kid.

"Dad, were you in Auschwitz too?"

"No, we were in the ghetto."

"The what?"

My father explained to me what the ghetto was and how he'd been there with his parents.

"Are there ghettos in Poland now?" I asked.

"No, you don't have to be scared."

I sighed with relief, because I'd been terrified that although I'd managed to deal with the camp, the ghetto might not be so easy. My dad and grandparents had been lucky and made it out of there. When he was three, my dad spent a year living in a cellar. He came out sometimes, but only at night. Things remained that way until the moment my grandpa heard a voice through the floor: we know you're hiding Jews. He didn't hear what came next. They waited for the visitor to leave the house, then fled a few minutes later.

"Dad, where are your grandparents?" I asked. I already knew that the ladder of children, parents and grandparents was the normal family structure.

"After the war my grandma left for America, and my grandpa was killed in the war."

"Did the Germans find him?"

"Grandpa was a teacher, one of his own Polish school-kids turned him in."

When you're only a few years old, it's easier to accept positive information. I already knew the Germans were bad, but I couldn't understand why Poles were helping them.

"Did that schoolkid not like your grandpa?"

"He didn't like Jews."

"Any of them?"

"Any of them."

"Would he have not liked me either?"

That was always the moment when my parents cut the conversation short. They did their best to change the subject subtly enough that I wouldn't notice. Or so they thought, but I was on to them. I could sense I ought to back off, but more and more often, I kept coming back to it.

"Do all Poles dislike all Jews?" I asked, gnawing at the subject.

"Some do, and sometimes most do."

That "sometimes" was hard to understand.

"Do they like them least in the winter?"

"The last time they stopped liking them was in the spring, and it lasted many months."

When the Arab countries attacked Israel in 1967, the Soviet Union supported the attackers. Poland, as part of the communist bloc, was by definition on the Soviet side.

That was all it took. June 1967 became the start of yet another wave of antisemitism, which reached its culmination in March 1968. An extreme nationalist faction gained the upper hand in the ruling party and unleashed an antisemitic witch hunt. Between March 1968 and 1970, over 13,000 Polish citizens with Jewish backgrounds left the country. Before that, they were thrown out of their jobs and universities, their apartments were confiscated, and they were stripped of their dignity. They scattered around the world, their jobs left vacant. People could get a promotion, take over someone's lovely apartment or simply feel the satisfaction of being a truer Pole than the Polish Jews.

The expelled went mainly to Israel, Sweden, Denmark and the United States. Departing retirees were stripped of their pensions, researchers were forbidden from bringing along the diplomas that proved their academic status. Masters, doctorates and post-doctoral work were all cut short.

The vast majority of these exiles considered themselves Poles, but the only country where they couldn't be Poles was in Poland. There were some who for decades to come never spoke Polish or even thought about travelling to Poland.

The communist government put an embargo on their existence; they became personae non gratae. They were not allowed into the country to visit ill parents, and later were forbidden entry for funerals. They were turned away from ferries, airports and road border crossings. The Polish intelligence services were effective enough that it didn't help to change your surname. They were disdained, and no power could have caused the gates at the border to open.

"Dad, why didn't we leave Poland?"

"That's a longer conversation."

"Then we'd better get started."

"On 8 March 1968, your mum had a meeting at the Academy of Fine Arts on Krakowskie Przedmieście. When thugs posing as worker activists started bludgeoning students at the University of Warsaw, some of the thugs got into the grounds of the academy too. Your mum phoned me at the department to say she'd got out through a window and she was safe now. At that moment, I was terrified. I was terrified for you and for your mother Daniela. That was the first time I thought seriously about leaving Poland. Plenty of people I knew, the ones who'd decided to leave, were encouraging me to go. They were sure with my professional status I'd have no trouble finding a job. Daniela didn't want to go, but she said: if you want to leave, then why don't we go to France? She spoke French fluently, she had family there, as well as some close friends of her parents, so for her it would be acceptable. Not for me. I was afraid of old civilisations, congealed societies where you're still a new-comer after 30 years. And anyone new is always an outsider. I didn't want that for you, or for us either. I believed we had to go to a young civilisation, like Australia or Canada."

"You didn't consider Israel?"

"No."

"Why didn't we leave in the end? What happened?"

"At a certain point I realised I was only alive because my parents had saved me during the war. If not for them, I'd never have survived in the ghetto or the Aryan hiding spots. In 1968 my dad was 65, and mum was over 70. They couldn't travel any more. I couldn't leave them. I knew I had to be here for when they needed me. Daniela and I made the final decision together. And we stayed. At that same time, we decided you couldn't be alone, and we made up our minds to have another kid."

"Was mum relieved?"

"There was no feeling relieved in those days. I told my father we'd made the decision to stay. At first he looked heartbroken, because he thought we should have got out.

'Why are you doing this?' he asked. And as I explained it to him, something started getting through. I think, in time, he was really grateful to us."

In 1968 I was two years old and I didn't leave. My parents lost most of their community and stayed in a country they no longer had any illusions about. In 1970 my brother was born.

In 1974 I went to primary school. At the start of the year my parents had a chat with my teacher. They asked if us not going to church would cause problems. She said not for the time being. The trouble would start when all the kids were having their first communions. She was right. It turned out that I was the only kid out of my whole year not taking communion. I picked a bad strategy from the start, though even in retrospect I haven't got the shadow of a doubt that there was no good one to pick. I held fast to what I'd learned at home, that humans were descended from apes. The Darwinian world didn't suit the Poland of May 1975. "Catch the Jew!", "Jew-hunt!" the other kids would shout at me. They were dangerous, because the instant I heard them I had to run, while dozens of kids, everyone within earshot – both boys and girls – chased after me.

By November we'd moved to a new area and I was going to a new school. I now had plenty of experience and knew the topic of Jewishness could be unsafe for me.

When my brother started school, I reported to my father:

9

"Dad, I checked. There are a few kids in his year not taking communion, we don't have to be afraid."

"Dad, do you remember how when we lived in France in the 80s, you tried to get us to stay?"

"No."

"Yeah. You even had us vote on it."

"That's true. I thought it couldn't only be up to me whether we stayed or went back."

"As we were leaving Poland I was sure we'd return."

"I wanted a shared decision, by Daniela, you boys and me. If you two had wanted to stay I'm sure we would have. I was ready to consider a move if you expressed the desire."

"Mum wanted to go back."

"I did, too."

"So did I, but Marcin was ten and I begged him to say he wanted to go back too. I was afraid the vote would be a tie. I thought you wanted to stay, and I knew Marcin had started feeling comfortable there."

"I considered a lot of options. My mum had passed away, dad had a new wife. The situation was different from '68. I was waiting for you boys' votes."

"You remember the conversation we had about anti-semitism on the way to France? We were driving in the Lada and you said that in France I didn't have to worry about something bad happening to me because I was Jewish. I already had a few tough experiences behind me. Tough enough that you even decided to move to a different area so I'd have it easier."

"I'd already spent at least a year and a half in France and I knew that the antisemitism over there was alive and well."

"But you told me it would be better."

"Because there it's less open, more beneath the surface."

"Right after we arrived, someone planted a bomb near the synagogue on rue Copernic in Paris. The French prime minister, Raymond Barre, said the attack killed such-and-such a number of Jews as well as such-and-such a number of innocent French people. Do you remember that?"

"Yes, and I remember you getting scared at the time."

"It wasn't the attack itself that scared me, it was how your promise had gone up in smoke. When we talked about it, you said you were very sorry, but it turned out what you'd told me wasn't true."

"But what else could I have said?"

Over three million Jews lived in pre-war Poland. After the war, and the return of those who'd survived by fleeing into the Soviet Union, the Jewish community numbered around 240,000 people. The ones who went back to their homes were not welcomed with open arms. Waiting for them were disarmingly frank neighbours: "What did you come back for?" "I see Hitler didn't finish his job." Pogroms (in July 1946, ethnic Poles in Kielce killed 37 Jewish Holocaust survivors and seriously injured 35) and arson committed against Jewish orphanages sparked a flight from Poland. By 1952 the Jewish community numbered only 70,000. Further waves of emigration took place during the post-Stalinist "Thaw" – between 1955 and 1960, another 51,000 left the country.

Just before the Solidarity movement was founded in 1980, the size of the Jewish community was estimated at 7,000.

In 2017 I had one of my last conversations with my dad.

"Dad, when did your 1968 end?"

"Well, son, the year ends in December, but I'm guessing that's not your question."

"You know full well what I'm asking."

"I used to think it ended sometime in the mid-70s."

"And what do you think now?"

"That it hasn't ended yet."

"That's a sad thing to say."

"Very sad."

Returning to the present, I owe my readers a few words about the current situation in Poland. On 27 January 2018, on the exact anniversary of the liberation of the Auschwitz-Birkenau concentration camp, the Polish parliament passed an amendment to the Institute of National Remembrance Act. Without going into detail, I'll write only about its intentions and the legal instrument the new legislation granted. The Polish justice system was empowered to prosecute anyone stating facts contradictory to the historical narrative endorsed by the government. It became illegal to mention Polish participation in the murder of the Jewish population during the Second World War. This despite the fact that documents in the archives of that same Institute of National Remembrance confirm many such cases.

The amendment thrust Poland into a diplomatic dispute with Israel and the United States. The Polish government responded to their words of outrage with a campaign about an anti-Polish Jewish conspiracy. The dam burst and a wave of reprehensible rhetoric inundated the public sphere. And those who played the antisemitism card saw their votes increase.

It was amid this very atmosphere that we observed the anniversary of my country's most recent antisemitic explosion.

The political slogans in Poland are virtually identical to the ones Donald Trump voiced in his presidential campaigns. The Polish version of "Make America Great Again" is "Poland Rising from its Knees". In reality, it was Polish antisemitism that rose from its knees.

In March 2018, on the 50th anniversary of the antisemitic campaign, I published a collection of conversations titled *The Book of Exodus*, some of which are included in this essay. The subjects are Jews affected by the events of March 1968. It enjoyed a great deal of attention and I set off on a promotional tour.

"We'd like to welcome to our library Mr Mikołaj Grynberg, a photographer, writer, and – I'll say something I've always wanted to say, and add that I'm not embarrassed to say it – a Jew."

A small city, in central Poland. The moderator's introduction from the very beginning divides the room into Jewish me and Polish everyone else.

A man in a sweater speaks up from the third row.

"Seeing as you've come to visit us, why don't you tell us how come you guys have got that POLIN Museum of the History of Polish Jews, but you didn't even put Korczak[1] in it. He was your guy, wasn't he? You people are always so hopeless."

I glance at the moderator – no reaction.

"Or why don't you tell us about Jews in the commie secret police?"

I ask the moderator if this is how our conversation is going to go. The moderator says nothing. She seems at a loss, but she says nothing.

The man in the sweater spreads his wings.

"Mr Grynberg, let's be honest with one another, you're not a Pole. I am, but you're not and we both know that perfectly well, don't we?"

Now the moderator isn't even pretending to lead the event, she's sitting passively beside me at the table. I don't know why she's smiling. Maybe from stress, or maybe the event is going just as she planned. Hard to tell. I ask the audience whether what the man in the sweater is saying is acceptable. All of them – mainly women, holding glasses of rose-hip tea, courtesy of the library – are staring at their shoes, but mutter that it's okay. I ask the man in the sweater what brings him to our event, and he replies without coaxing.

---

1. Janusz Korczak was a writer and Polish-Jewish educator, who went to his death in Treblinka with 200 children from the orphanage he ran.

"I wanted to see a Jew."

I didn't leave the event, though I should have. I didn't punch him in the face, though I badly wanted to. My wife was in the room and luckily it occurred to me that if I did, she'd have to extract me from the police station. I didn't punch the man in the face because I was surprised at how quickly the incident had escalated. To this day I'm sorry I didn't.

The event moved into a second phase. I made an attempt to take control and – with the moderator's silent agreement – I read a story from my book *Rejwach*, one about a woman who's a passive-aggressive, antisemitic schoolteacher. When I finished, the man in the sweater, without batting an eye, didn't let up:

"So you couldn't have written in your own language?"

I pushed through to the end of the event. It was obvious to me that the values of the past had returned. The stories my parents and grandparents had told me were unfolding before my eyes. In Poland it was again possible to make aggressively antisemitic statements with the silent consent of those present.

A few months later I got an email of apology from the woman moderating that event. She asked my forgiveness for putting me in that situation and thanked me for behaving politely. "Politely", meaning I didn't storm out, but instead courteously heard out his impudence? "Politely", meaning I didn't force her to take responsibility for the course of the event she was running? And last of all, "politely", because I didn't protest when she excluded me from the community of Poles? I think "politely" only meant that I allowed her to passively observe everything that happened.

That event was difficult, but it taught me a great deal.

I get event requests in various ways, most often by email. I relatively quickly understood that instead of writing back, it was worth calling.

"How nice of you to call back, so will you come see us? What do you mean the date doesn't work for you? You people are always like this, isn't it enough that we're inviting you...?"

To be absolutely clear, I asked if by "you people" she meant writers.

"Don't be ridiculous", replied the lady from the community centre, "we both know who I'm talking about."

I didn't go.

Nor did I go to a library in southern Poland. Instead of writing back, I phoned.

"Another date's out of the question, we want you to come in March because it is the anniversary of March '68. Any later and you're of no interest to us."

The telephone is a fantastic invention; it's spared me many uncomfortable situations. I'd like to say I have a hard time believing what people will come out with. That was true the first few times; after that I had no trouble believing, I just felt sad.

Two days earlier I'd been at an event where someone told me I was making money in Poland that I'd later export to you-know-where. I was already feeling a little tired, or maybe the weight of my experiences was finally pulling me under. So suddenly, before I could think, a third strategy popped into my head. I stood up and, in concise and vivid Polish, let him know exactly what I thought about the level of discourse he'd so politely proposed.

"All right, maybe I got a little carried away, but you've got to see where I'm coming from."

I did not.

"So what, we can't have a conversation? You people are always the same, you're never willing to communicate."

That's exactly how we are; we don't talk with anyone manifesting some unjustified sense of superiority.

Marching through Poland's streets today are the same organisations that forbade my grandparents from studying in Poland.

FRANCE'S MODEL
MINORITY

Natasha Lehrer

IN NOVEMBER 2018, a new French protest movement was born. The fury of the protestors – who took their name from the yellow vests drivers are legally obliged to keep in their cars in case of an accident – was triggered by a sharp rise in the price of petrol, disproportionately affecting millions of people living in towns and villages inadequately served by public transport, who depend on their cars for getting to work or taking their children to school. The protests rapidly came to be seen as a new emblem of a divided country, highlighting the vast economic gulf that lies between large, prosperous cities like Paris, and France's hinterlands, where people struggle to get by on their monthly pay cheques.

Even after President Macron had withdrawn the price hike and broken his promise to Brussels to bring down public spending by offering billions of euros to benefit the least well off, the sporadically violent weekly protests continued, burning out only when France's strict pandemic lockdown came into force in early March 2020, almost a year and a half after they had begun.

The Gilets Jaunes, a predominantly – but not entirely – white, male phenomenon, drawing support from left, right and centre, appeared not to be remotely concerned with immigration or race. Nonetheless, within a month of the movement coming into being, familiar and disturbing antisemitic tropes were beginning to emerge among their supporters. In truth, to note it feels almost mundane, so frequently does the antisemitic trope appear on the streets in France, even when there is no apparent link with whatever is being protested.

At first the reports were anecdotal. One Saturday evening in December 2018, a journalist returning home on the Paris metro witnessed a verbal attack on an elderly Jewish woman by two young men still wearing their yellow jackets, on their way home from the protest. After they made the "quenelle" gesture (a hybrid gesture crossing a lowered Nazi salute and a bras d'honneur, the French equivalent of sticking up two fingers, popularised over the last decade by the comedian Dieudonné M'bala M'bala, who has been convicted multiple times of inciting antisemitic hatred), they insulted her, told her the gas chambers had never existed and praised Vichy, the French collaborationist government during the Second World War.

It was a single episode, but hard to ignore. Others followed. One Saturday afternoon in February 2019, one of the country's most prominent, and controversial, public intellectuals, the Jewish philosopher Alain Finkielkraut – who, ironically enough, had been a vocal supporter of the movement since its inception – was verbally attacked as he left his apartment; a group of passing Gilets Jaunes called him a "filthy Zionist bastard" and began chanting familiar far-right slogans, "France belongs to us" and "We are the people." The incident, which was filmed by a passer-by, shows a number of men screaming, "You're going to die and go to hell."

Events like these took place week after week. In January 2020, during one of the last Saturday marches in Paris before the country locked down, an orthodox Jewish family who had come out onto their balcony was whistled at, jeered and catcalled by the crowd; some people, carrying Palestinian flags, were filmed yelling, *Rentrez chez vous!* (Go back to where you came from) as they passed by. The Gilets Jaunes was evolving into a populist movement, leaning increasingly towards the extremes on both the left and the right, and proving to be an incubator for a pernicious and increasingly open expression of the kind of blatant antisemitic rhetoric that so often goes hand in hand with populism.

For many years, traditional white, often Catholic, antisemitism has been considered to be in retreat in France. Even Marine Le Pen, whose father Jean-Marie, an unashamed and vocal antisemite, founded the National Front, the party she now leads (renamed in 2018 Rassemblement National or National Rally), abandoned it during the last presidential campaign in 2017 in favour of trying to court Jewish voters with her anti-Muslim rhetoric. For over a decade, some of the most shocking antisemitic acts in France have been committed by people known in French parlance as "descended from North African immigration", and others who have been radicalised by Islamic State, with attacks on people, synagogues or other sites such as cemeteries usually triggered by flare-ups in the Middle East.

The 2017 murder of 65-year-old Sarah Halimi, who was savagely beaten before being thrown from the third-floor balcony of her home in a working-class neighbourhood of Paris by a young man of North African origin, was horrifically typical of a bleak roll call of victims since the turn of the millennium. Although more Jews have been murdered in the US in the last three years than in the last decade in France, the French tally is nevertheless shocking. Since the beginning of this century, casualties include: 23-year-old DJ Sébastien Selam in 2003, stabbed to death by a childhood friend; 23-year-old phone salesman Ilan Halimi, kidnapped and murdered by the self-styled "Gang of Barbarians" in 2006; three Jewish schoolchildren and a teacher shot in a school playground in Toulouse in 2012; four hostages, of whom three were Jewish, shot at the Hypercacher supermarket in January 2015, two days after the murder of 12 people at the Charlie Hebdo offices; Sarah Halimi; and 85-year-old Holocaust survivor Mireille Knoll, killed in her apartment by a neighbour and an accomplice in 2018. And that's not to mention the regular verbal and physical harassment of Jewish adults and children as they go about their lives, the victims of break-ins and robberies and violent attacks on people and property that are almost commonplace in certain neighbourhoods of Paris and other cities. In Lyon, a rabbi's 14-month-old baby daughter was burned after acid was poured into her stroller, parked in the hall of the family's apartment building. An orthodox Jewish woman told me that she did not allow her husband or young sons to go out wearing their kippot – skullcaps – for fear that they would be attacked. Her husband stood beside her with a Knicks baseball cap wedged firmly on his head, concealing the kippah underneath. According to official police statistics, antisemitic acts rose by 74 per cent in 2018, and by a more modest but still significant 27 per cent in 2019. Well over half of all racist attacks in France target Jews, even though they number less than 1 per cent of the population.

The police were at first hesitant to acknowledge that Sarah Halimi's killers had been motivated by antisemitism, just as they were after the murders of Sébastien Selam and Ilan Halimi (who shared a surname but was not related), as James McAuley noted in the *Washington Post*: "French authorities have often hesitated to formally ascribe a motivation of 'antisemitism' to attacks on Jews in recent years. This has been a point of contention between Jewish leaders and the French government. The Sarah Halimi killing became a national scandal when authorities initially declined to investigate it as an antisemitic attack, despite her family's testimony that the suspect had confronted her with verbal slurs on a regular basis."

It might seem, to a casual observer, that the avoidance of ascribing antisemitic motives for the murder of Jews could be attributed to failings within the criminal justice system or even evidence of institutional antisemitism. In fact, such reticence when it comes to labelling crimes of racial hatred is embedded in republican ideals of equality and "universalism", whose roots go back to the French Revolution. In the pre-revolutionary ancien régime, the circumstances of a person's birth dictated their station in life, whether peasant, landowner or aristocrat. After the revolution, the inclusive status of "citizen" was created, granting full and equal rights to all Frenchmen (notably, for well over a century, universalism did not include women within its purview). This means, in effect, that racial, ethnic or religious difference is legally erased from a person's identity. The state is, supposedly, colour-blind, and accords rights to individuals, not on the basis of any group identity or ethnic or religious particularity. (Though it is illegal to collect data on race or religion, this was not the case during the Second World War, when the word "juif" was stamped on the identity cards of Jews, making the job of the French police charged with arresting them considerably more straightforward. This blot on French history, which was not to be fully acknowledged until the 1990s, is another reason for the continued taboo on identifying French citizens as belonging to a particular minority.)

In the years immediately following the French Revolution, Jews were the first minority to be fully emancipated, in an ongoing process, on condition that they agreed to put the laws of their country above those of their religion, thus abiding by the laws of the new Republic. The acceptance of Jews as citizens is both the cornerstone of modern French-Jewish identity, and a foundation stone in the edifice of French republicanism. As historian Maurice Samuels makes clear, "Despite representing a tiny minority of the French population, Jews have played an out-sized role in the French political imagination since 1789, shaping the ways in which universalism has been theorised and implemented."

Universalism could, in a country that at least in its own imagination is fiercely secular, legitimately be called the national religion. Yet the constant recourse in both political and media discourse to "republican values", however lofty they may be in theory, has led to the impoverishment of the language needed to address very concrete problems of antisemitism and racism. Debates around religious or ethnic identity and prejudice that have been going on for decades in English-speaking countries remain virtually taboo in France. The term "race" was actually removed from the constitution in 2018, on the high-minded grounds that the term is "outdated" and "unhelpful". Of course, republican rhetoric and the insistence on purportedly "universal" values cannot erase the reality of racism; rather, they render it spectacularly difficult to discuss.

On 28 March 2018, five days after Mireille Knoll's body was found in her burned-out apartment, some 30,000 people marched through the streets of Paris in silent homage. The march was notable for being the first time since 1990 – when as many as 200,000 demonstrators across the country denounced the desecration of the Jewish cemetery of Carpentras – that significant numbers of people of all faiths and backgrounds gathered in Paris in solidarity with Jews. Social media was awash with various high-profile Jewish figures declaring that they were not marching because Knoll was Jewish but because she could have been "anyone's" grandmother: in the words of the rabbi Delphine Horvilleur, "I dream of a France that knows that her grandmother was murdered... and not just 'mine'. A nation that stands up to horror, and does not simply offer condolences to a 'community'." Horvilleur's sentiment was well-meaning, but troubling: Knoll was not killed because she was a grandmother, but because she was a Jew. Not everybody's grandmother is Jewish. Horvilleur neatly, if inadvertently, summed up the contortions that French people, Jews in particular, make as they try to articulate the problem of acknowledging the specificity of racism without acknowledging the specificity of race.

Two years later, the reliably knotty question of how to counter racism in a country that refuses to collect data on ethnicity was infused with new urgency as the relaxing of the lockdown in the wake of the first wave of coronavirus in France coincided with the emergence of the global Black Lives Matter movement. (Limited statistics are collected based on the "nationality at birth" of an individual or their parents or grandparents, as a senior demographer at Insee, the French National Institute of Statistics and

Economic Studies, was at pains to point out recently.) The classic republican refusal to recognise race found itself up against vast public fury after the June 2020 judicial review exonerating the police of guilt for the death of a 24-year-old Black man, Adama Traoré, in police custody in 2016, which uncannily prefigured the asphyxiation by a police officer of George Floyd in Minneapolis. Large demonstrations took place in several French cities, protesting police violence and triggering the faltering beginnings of a difficult conversation about institutional racism, slavery and France's colonial history. The continuing dogged refusal in France in parts of the media (the reports of his death at the time completely failed to mention that Traoré was Black) much of the political class and all of the legal system to acknowledge even the possibility of systemic racism in parts of French society renders this conversation agonisingly complicated. However, some politicians, even on the more conservative end of the spectrum, are beginning publicly to recognise the extent of systemic racism in France. In June 2020, human rights ombudsman and former minister of culture Jacques Toubon published his report on systemic racism. It can hardly be emphasised enough how radical it is, in a country that has up until now refused to budge from its official colour-blind position, to acknowledge, in the words of the report, that "those of foreign origin or perceived as such are disadvantaged when it comes to access to employment or housing, and are more exposed to unemployment, insecurity, poor housing, police checks, poor health, and educational inequalities".

◈ ◈ ◈

In her magisterial work *The Figural Jew: Politics and Identity in Postwar French Thought*, Sarah Hammerschlag argues that in every era of political change in France, the negative characteristics associated with Jews also change. "As a figure in the rhetoric of the 1789 revolution, [the Jew] represented the negative image of the Enlightenment ideal." Even when Jews were emancipated almost immediately after the revolution – the first Jewish community in the world to achieve political emancipation – Hammerschlag argues that it remained the case that "whatever the political ideal, the Jew was its antithesis". For progressive reformers, the Jew was "a tribal remnant of an outmoded culture, a figure trenchantly attached to backward customs and superstition... a symbol of particularism, which the Revolution was meant to overcome". But by the end of the 19th century, leaders of the Catholic right, including notably the journalist Édouard Drumont, known as France's "pope of antisemitism", were identifying the cosmopolitan Jew as the "secret victor" of the 1789 revolution.

In the years leading up to the Second World War, the negative trope of the "rootless" Jew had become the antithesis of all that sovereign culture and nationalism represented as fascism took hold in the country. A quarter of a century later, during the student uprising of May '68, the Jews' outsider status had evolved into "a resistance to an abstract humanism by its very exceptionality and the foil of foreignness to a French identity built on roots"; when activist-turned-politician Daniel Cohn-Bendit led fellow students in the chant "We are all German Jews", he was in effect refusing the terms of identification with the available political structures of power. The figure of the Jew now represented "destabilisation itself".

Hammerschlag deftly illustrates how for over two centuries the idea of the Jew has had a moral and political significance in the way French identity is constructed and bolstered at different historical moments. When, in the wake of the Charlie Hebdo/Hypercacher massacres in 2015, then prime minister Manuel Valls declared that "France would not be France without the Jews", what sounded like a platitude was in fact its opposite: the emancipation of the Jews was literally one of the defining characteristics of the post-revolutionary Republic. Not only that: as Maurice Samuels reminds us, Jews were able, thanks to France's "rigorous policy of equality and neutrality", to penetrate "the highest levels of the education and political establishments much sooner than Jews in any other country".

For two centuries, Jews in France – who today comprise the third-largest Jewish population in the world, after Israel and the United States – have, in effect, been the "model minority", against whom all other minorities must be measured, as in the words of prominent Jewish philosopher Bernard-Henri Lévy: "French Jews, since the time of Napoleon, have erased from their body of thought all that could be in strong conflict with the law of their country. The Muslims have not done it yet. The Christians did it, but only very late. The depth of Judaism does not come into conflict with the idea of the French Republic."

The Holocaust, during which the collaborationist Vichy government deported some 75,000 Jews from France to their deaths (of whom fewer than 3,000 survived), engendered a complicated Jewish identity in the post-war era. The prevailing narrative has long been that in the two decades after the war the Jews accepted de Gaulle's project of national healing, which encouraged them not to see themselves as having experienced a distinct and specific trauma: what historian Leora Auslander has called "a quiescent fidelity to republicanism". But this too has been challenged by historians such as Daniella Doron, who stresses the nuanced complexity of French-Jewish identity right up to the present day, contesting the image of the assimilated Jew of the post-Enlightenment era, and pointing out that even those who reached the highest echelons of French society, whether in political administration or commerce, "balanced their loyalty to republican universalism with continued Jewish particularity". Indeed, beginning in the 1960s, with the arrival of 300,000 Jews from France's former colonies and protectorates, primarily Algeria, Tunisia and Morocco, there has been a well-documented and significant uptick in the Jewish embrace of community politics, as these Sephardi populations began to use communal organisations to express an assertive collective identity in defiance of the republican model of French-Jewish citizenship. This rise in communitarian politics has been at least passively condoned by the state since the 1990s. During his presidency, Nicolas Sarkozy expanded Holocaust education in schools, leading to an outcry on the part of some activists that slavery was not similarly prominent in the secondary education programme. It is a long-established tradition that the country's president and other important ministers attend the annual dinner held by the CRIF, the main Jewish umbrella organisation, while there is no regular presence at any official event organised by other minority groups. For complex historical reasons, to do with both French guilt about the Holocaust and the longstanding relationship of Jews with the Republic, Jews are essentially the one minority group that is permitted this level of state representation in a country supposedly rigorously opposed to manifestations of minority identity.

At the same time, Jews have long been at the forefront of broad social justice movements in France; the dawn of the anti-racist movement dates back to the 1920s and 30s when, in the aftermath of the Dreyfus affair, the LICA (International League Against Anti-Semitism), the forerunner of the LICRA (League Against Racism and Anti-Semitism) was set up. SOS-Racisme was co-founded in 1984 by a Jew, Julien Dray. As historian Emmanuel Debono explains, both the LICRA and MRAP (Movement Against Racism and For Friendship Between Peoples), founded in 1949, played a major role in militating for the anti-racism laws that were eventually adopted in 1972, and were highly influential in defining anti-racist discourse in France, drawing on the universalist paradigm of fighting racism by integrating every citizen as an individual into the body politic. Indeed, in the wake of the recent demonstrations, France's main Jewish organisations' response has been to declare that "they will continue to fight racism alongside their traditional partners", including SOS-Racisme, rather than aligning themselves, as have a few high-profile individuals such as senator Esther Benbassa, with the Traoré protest movement. Francis Kalifat, head of the CRIF, told the Israeli newspaper *Haaretz* in July 2020, "I think what needs to be done now is intensify our actions against racism, push more for change, denounce all discrimination. The universal fight against racism can bring results."

There are many militants on the frontline of anti-racist action in France who would disagree with Kalifat's statement, which manages to be both banal and contentious. Since the beginning of the 21st century there has been a growing sense on both right and left that in what is today one of the most multicultural countries in the world, albeit one whose constitution and legal system remain defiantly colour-blind, the traditional model of universalism is breaking down. The arguments from the left claim that universalism is a form of forced assimilation, erasing difference in favour of conservative cultural norms, while those on the right worry that the country is becoming increasingly communautaire, fragmented into minority communities who defend their religious or ethnic affiliation above pride in their national identity.

The far right has traditionally opposed universalism for its undermining of France's traditional Catholic roots. However, as historian Emile Chabal explains, in the last three decades even the far-right National Front "has selectively deployed the transformative narrative of republicanism as a way of exhorting the French people to protect their distinctive national 'qualities'." This has led to "an extensive reinterpretation of one of republicanism's core values, laicité", which requires that the secular rules of the republic take precedence over religious law, and has evolved to mean that all manifestations of religious affiliation must take place exclusively in the private sphere. This brief explanation does not do justice to the protean nature of laicité, which has been used over recent years to justify decrees promulgated by governments of both left and right banning Muslim mothers from wearing headscarves on school trips or allowing mayors to refuse to provide alternatives to pork in their towns' school canteens. With the ghastly beheading of Samuel Paty in October 2020 after he showed his class of 13-year-olds a caricature of the prophet Mohammed, the French found themselves being strongly criticised at an international level for the state's unbending support of laicité as being absolutely central to French values. Where a century ago laicité was most strongly associated with progressive politics, deployed in muscular opposition to Catholic conservatism, it is now those who cleave to the centre-right, often labelled neo-republicans, who most strongly adhere to its ideology, while the far right has increasingly been co-opting its vocabulary to call for draconian limits on immigration, claiming that immigrants, particularly those from Muslim majority countries, do not respect its hallowed dogma.

In 2021, former journalist Eric Zemmour emerged as one of the most popular potential candidates for president. His Berber-Jewish parents immigrated to France during the Algerian War. A far-right provocateur who is mainly known for his sulphurous contributions to a popular nightly television chat show, Zemmour began an enthusiastic campaign to rehabilitate the wartime Vichy government, which he claims – against all the historical evidence – refused to collaborate in the deportation of French-born Jews and were in fact trying to save Jewish lives. That, plus his hate speech against Muslims, for which he has received several suspended sentences, and his anti-immigration rhetoric, plays well in a conservative population that sees "traditional French values" as being under threat.

The philosopher Alain Finkielkraut, who was targeted by the Gilets Jaunes with antisemitic abuse, remains a constant and controversial presence in the debate around integration, identity and universalism in France. Virulently opposed to any whisper of identity politics, he has increasingly become the face of a universalism that is hostile not only to multiculturalism but also to certain minority identities themselves. Finkielkraut's rhetoric, which links anti-racist movements with both racism and antisemitism, perfectly illustrates the neurosis of the traditional conservative universalism pitted against the new identitarian anti-racism. In the words of Emmanuel Debono, in an interview with *Le Monde* in June 2020, "We are emerging from the historic struggle for general emancipation and laws that are supposed to apply equally to everyone. We are moving away from the idea of a common cause."

Today, Jews find themselves on the faultline of anti-racist activism, as universalism, the basis of their emancipation and an ideology to which they have, largely, loyally cleaved for two centuries, is now being loudly repudiated by militant anti-racist collectives, who argue that it is inadequate for the purpose of fighting inequality in what their supporters believe to be a society deeply riven by systemic racism. True to Hammerschlag's observation that the negative characteristics associated with Jews shift at moments of political change, today the mainstream Jewish population finds itself sidelined from the current debate on racism, at a time when Jews are still frequent targets of antisemitism. Long-standing tradition, and implicit and explicit positioning within official state memorials, including state representation at annual Holocaust memorial ceremonies, has led to a belief among many Black leaders that Jewish history is dealt with far more favourably than Black and Muslim history. The last two decades have seen a bitter and contentious debate develop over "competitive victimhood", pitting the traumatic memory of the Holocaust against both the traumatic memory of slavery and the more recent deeply divisive legacy of the bitter and bloody Algerian War. One unfortunate effect of the competitive memory discourse has been an increase in antisemitic rhetoric, with a number of activists in other minority communities claiming that the official recognition the Jewish community receives is evidence of Jewish "power" or "privilege". But what this rhetoric fails to acknowledge is that whatever recognition the Jewish community enjoys today, it was hard-won over years of organisation and campaigning within the Jewish community itself, which struggled for decades to break the post-war silence around the role of the collaborationist Vichy government in the deportation of Jews to Nazi death camps. The same level of organisation is now materialising in other minority communities. The Foundation for the Memory of Slavery (its name, not uncoincidentally, echoing the Foundation for the Memory of the Shoah), officially launched in February 2020 by its instigator, former prime minister Jean-Marc Ayrault, will, it is hoped, go some way to genuinely addressing these concerns.

In 1998, historian Paula Hyman presciently observed "how France and her Jews together negotiate the balance between equality and particularism will determine the contours of Jewish life in France in the 21st century". It has become urgently apparent that how France deals with the challenge of ethnic and religious particularism of all minorities will determine the contours of French identity as a whole and the wider political landscape in the next few years. Until France accords similar levels of representation to minorities other than Jews, who have been historically, and to all intents and purposes remain, the only group allowed to be "different" within the "universal" republic, the perception of Jews as a privileged minority places them in a difficult, even potentially dangerous, position in a national landscape of fracturing and fractious identity politics.

LOOKING FOR AN ENEMY

Daniel Trilling

IN MAY 2010, more than half a million people voted for the British National Party (BNP). The result is still the highest-ever vote received by a fascist party in a UK general election. Nick Griffin, then leader of the BNP, was a veteran Holocaust denier with a criminal conviction for incitement to racial hatred. Antisemitic conspiracy theory was central to the world view of the party's founders, who were driven by their belief in a global Jewish plot to destroy the white race.

Yet the party only progressed when it attempted to conceal these views from the public. From the early 2000s onwards, it attracted support by talking about "identity" rather than race and focusing its rhetorical attacks on people whom the mainstream right frequently demonised: Muslims, asylum seekers and immigrants from eastern Europe.

Despite these tactics, within months of its success, the BNP had collapsed. Opinion polls suggested that there was in fact a much larger pool of potential support in the UK for the far right, and that many of these voters were put off by the BNP's thinly veiled neo-Nazism, which was easily exposed by journalists and anti-fascist campaigners. During the 2010 campaign, for instance, one former senior member revealed that candidates underwent media training in how to avoid questions about the Holocaust.

At the time, it seemed as if the BNP represented a trend that was on its way out. Indeed, the real beneficiaries of discontent on the right turned out to be the newer movements that had little or no association with antisemitic conspiracy theory. The UK Independence Party (UKIP), right-wing populists, made a show of banning anybody who had been a member of the BNP from joining. On the streets, the English Defence League (EDL), an anti-Muslim protest movement that emerged in 2009, claimed to oppose racism and prominently displayed Israeli flags at its demonstrations, supposedly as a symbol of solidarity with Jews. In a country with relatively low levels of open antisemitism, where explicitly antisemitic statements are generally seen as a death knell to a politician's career, it might have seemed as if even the far right was adapting to this reality.

More than ten years on, the situation is more complex, and more troubling. Fascist groups with antisemitism at their core have gained a new lease of life online and passed on their ideas to a new generation. In the UK, for instance, a series of recent trials has revealed the inner workings of National Action, a "revolutionary nationalist" group founded by former BNP members that has recruited among younger people and was connected to a plot to murder a Labour MP.

At the same time, the global rise of right-wing populism has been accompanied by an increase in both open antisemitism and the entry of far-right tropes into the mainstream that – at the very least – echo antisemitic conspiracy theory. Donald Trump has been a major catalyst, from his ascent to the US presidency to his departure. Research by the Anti-Defamation League, an American-Jewish campaign group, linked his presidential election campaign in 2016 to a sharp rise in antisemitic views posted on Twitter. In January 2021, among the images that spread worldwide of the fascists, conspiracy theorists and white supremacists who stormed the Capitol at the president's pleasure, was one of a man wearing a sweatshirt that bore the slogan "Camp Auschwitz".

British conservatives, some of whom spent four years basking in Trump's glow, were quick to distance themselves. But far-right themes have been leaking into UK politics too. In June 2020, for example, the former UKIP leader Nigel Farage was criticised by Jewish community groups for repeatedly making claims about "globalist" plots to undermine national governments, which they claimed amounted to antisemitic "dog whistles". Even some prominent Conservative MPs, trying to co-opt the populist revolt in the wake of the Brexit referendum, have at times made claims that echo infamous antisemitic campaigns of the 20th century, positioning themselves as the defenders of ordinary, decent people against a rootless, cosmopolitan elite.

Far-right politics is structurally incapable of cutting its links with antisemitism. For the most extreme parts of this milieu, it will most likely always remain fundamental. Other, apparently more moderate politicians who trade in far-right ideas will tend to behave in ways that mimic the shape and tone of antisemitism, even if they disavow it. An examination of the particular role played by antisemitic conspiracy theory within the far right shows us why this way of doing politics is so dangerous – not only for Jewish communities, but for everyone.

◈ ◈ ◈

A study by the Institute for Jewish Policy Research in 2017 found that the proportion of people who openly express antisemitic views in the UK is relatively consistent across the political spectrum – and relatively low – except among people who define themselves as "very right-wing". Here, the proportion is two to four times higher than in the general population.

A common-sense explanation for this would be that since people with far-right views are likely to be prejudiced against a range of groups, it follows that they are more likely to be antisemitic too. But this doesn't tell the whole story. "The far right" is an umbrella term for a range of radical right-wing movements – including fascists, populists and single-issue campaigners – that promote heavily exclusionary forms of nationalism. Not all of these currents are motivated primarily by antisemitic conspiracy theory, but it has remained a constant among the most extreme of these groups that draw on explicitly fascist ideas, even when antisemitism proves a major barrier to recruiting members or attracting votes.

To take the BNP as an example, the belief that Jews were attempting to undermine the white race through mass immigration underpinned the party's founding ideology. The BNP was established in the early 1980s by John Tyndall, a veteran neo-Nazi who had led a series of other groups including the National Front. "Jewry is a world pest wherever it is found," Tyndall told an interviewer in 1964. "The Jews are more clever and more financially powerful than other people and have to be eradicated before they destroy the Aryan peoples."

Tyndall came from a tradition that sought explicitly to revive the ideas of the Nazis, applying them to a range of perceived social problems in post-war Britain. Its adherents saw race and nation as synonymous and their solutions involved the removal and destruction of people they categorised as racial enemies. From the 1960s onwards, the parties to which Tyndall belonged agitated chiefly around immigration to the UK from former colonies in Asia, the Caribbean and Africa. The BNP continued in this vein: in 1993, for instance, it won its first-ever seat in local government by exploiting the resentment of white residents of the Isle of Dogs in east London, who believed (wrongly) that their South Asian neighbours were being given priority for council housing.

Yet although the BNP increasingly hid its antisemitism from public view – particularly after Nick Griffin took over as party leader in the late 1990s, with a plan to sanitise its image in order to win more elections – the beliefs persisted. When I interviewed Griffin in 2011, he described the Holocaust as a "huge moral club" used to silence "anyone who asks questions of immigration". Denying or minimising the extent of the Holocaust is a priority for far-right antisemites, not only because it is the greatest warning about where this sort of politics leads, but because to many, remembering the Holocaust is itself evidence of a Jewish conspiracy: they believe that Jews have created a myth of genocide in order to stifle debate.

Such beliefs are remarkably consistent among ideologically committed neo-Nazis, across a range of cultural contexts, even when they are obviously out of step with the surrounding society. Typically, supporters and recruits are drawn in by engaging with public-facing campaigns that overlap with more mainstream right-wing themes, and are then gradually inducted into the core set of ideas, via private meetings and publications. As another long-term BNP member I interviewed in 2011 told me, one's "intellect" in what he called "nationalist" circles was measured "by the extent of your antisemitism and how much you understand the nature of the worldwide Jewish conspiracy".

The process still happens: the recent trial of the Greek

fascist movement Golden Dawn heard testimony from a series of former members who describe the same pattern of indoctrination. The counter-extremism researcher Julia Ebner has found similar processes at play, in undercover investigative work, among newer groups that recruit and coordinate online.

To understand why this might be the case, it's worth considering what fascism actually means. It is a notoriously slippery concept, but can be viewed as the most extreme form of nationalism, which offers a single solution to social conflict: purify your community. On the surface, fascist movements can look very different from one another, since they are appealing to different national communities, with different cultures and different histories. Not all have started off as antisemitic, but fascist movements of the past tended to become more so as they radicalised, while today antisemitism remains central to groups that try to keep Nazi ideas alive.

This is because fascist ideology attempts to gather together a set of disparate, often contradictory themes and give them coherence. The US author Chip Berlet provides a useful anatomy of the far right's world view, which he splits into four elements: "producerism", or the belief that the nation is held back by parasitical elites and a lazy under-class; demonisation and scapegoating; conspiracism; and an apocalyptic narrative. Political currents on the wider far right might only dwell on one or other of these themes – the QAnon movement for instance, a significant influence on the US right, is primarily conspiracist, while the now largely defunct EDL was mainly about the demonisation and scapegoating of Muslims – but fully developed fascist ideology brings them all together.

Think of the fasces, the ancient Roman symbol of authority that Mussolini's National Fascist Party, the first such mass movement, used as its logo. It is a bundle of sticks tied together with a leather strap. When assembled, it is apparently unbreakable, but without the strap the pieces fall apart. Fascism needs a binding agent, and for the most extreme parts of the far right, antisemitic conspiracy theory provides it – the belief that Jews are a malevolent, inhuman presence in the world whose workings are largely hidden from view.

Yet the story of the last decade has not been the return of fascism, in the sense described above. Instead, right-wing populist parties have been in the ascendant, surrounded by a loose and varied collection of other far-right agitators, some but not all of whom are fascists. What these different currents share, however, is a reliance on conspiracist thinking that at the very least echoes some deep-rooted antisemitic themes, even if this connection is obscured or, in some cases, vociferously denied.

Three common examples of this type of thinking are the accusation of "cultural Marxism", distorted claims about the philanthropist and currency speculator George Soros, and the "great replacement" conspiracy theory. Each of these has antisemitic roots. Cultural Marxism – the idea that left-wing ideology has a stranglehold on public institutions – began life on the US far right, as a conspiracy theory about the Frankfurt School, a circle of left-wing philosophers who fled Nazi Germany for New York in the 1930s. These philosophers, most of whom were Jewish, stood accused of fomenting a plot to undermine Christian-American values by warping young minds.

Soros, whose Open Society Foundations spend large amounts of money promoting anti-racist and pro-democracy causes around the world, has for many years been the target of conspiracy theories about the extent of his influence. In their most extreme versions, these theories evoke the well-worn stereotype of a manipulative, rootless Jewish financier: Soros is the child of a Hungarian-Jewish family who avoided deportation to Auschwitz in the 1940s by posing as Christians. The "great replacement" theory, meanwhile, holds that liberal elites are conspiring to deliberately undermine white-majority populations through mass immigration – a claim that has an obvious resemblance to the antisemitism that animated parties such as the BNP.

Yet in many instances today, the antisemitic connotations appear to have been discarded. To take "cultural Marxism" as an example, this idea gained international prominence when it was used by Anders Breivik as justification for the murder of 77 people in Norway in July 2011.

Breivik, setting a model for subsequent far-right terrorist attacks in different parts of the world, used the internet to maximise the impact of his actions, posting a video statement and a lengthy "manifesto" online shortly before he carried out the massacre. In his words, he acted to defend western civilisation from multiculturalism, an "anti-European hate ideology" orchestrated by "cultural Marxists", who had encouraged the Islamic "colonisation" of Europe. This had the hallmarks of classic far-right conspiracy theory – with a notable difference. In Breivik's world view, the plot to undermine the west came from Muslims, in connivance with the liberal left. Indeed, Breivik saw himself as a defender of Jews, and viewed the state of Israel as an outpost of civilisation in a hostile majority-Muslim region.

Breivik's actions may have stood out for their murderous violence, but his views were part of a wider current in far-right thought. He saw himself as part of the "counter-jihad" movement, a loose international network of anti-Muslim activists that developed in the wake of 9/11. The counter-jihad movement reframed a traditional far-right theme – a civilisational threat from an external enemy, aided by traitors from within – in terms that had potentially far wider appeal, since anti-Muslim racism is widespread and openly expressed in much of Europe and North America. These ideas helped shape a series of new groups, including the EDL.

Yet despite its apparent novelty, this strand of the far right has been no less conspiracy-minded. In 2018, I catalogued a week's worth of Facebook posts by "Tommy Robinson" (aka Stephen Yaxley-Lennon), the former figurehead of the EDL, who had gone on to become one of the English-speaking world's most prominent social media activists. The two dozen posts included links to stories about the "migrant invasion" of Europe, a piece attacking a prominent left-wing journalist, and claims that the mayor of London, Sadiq Khan, had allowed crime to run out of control. These were all familiar right-wing themes – some of the stories were taken from the *Daily Mail*, for instance – but with a particular framing: they amounted to an existential threat, political and media elites were allowing it to happen, and people who spoke out about it were silenced.

Among the far right, a conspiracy theory – one that blames a range of perceived ills on a nebulous, hidden, yet strangely powerful force – is always waiting to emerge, even if it sometimes isn't fully articulated. While some far-right groups continue to identify this hidden force as Jewish, they sit within a wider milieu in which the targets of blame may vary but the sense of conspiracy remains. In a recent survey of the far right, the linguist Ruth Wodak argues that in contexts where open antisemitism is regarded as socially unacceptable, historically antisemitic sentiments continue to be expressed in "coded" ways, such that the speaker may not even regard what they are saying as antisemitic. Wodak gives examples of particular claims about Jews – such as "Jews try to take advantage of having been victims in the Nazi era" – that echo older stereotypes about Jewish power and influence, but I would suggest that this coding works in another direction, too. Even when far-right movements appear to reject antisemitism, they cannot escape the pattern of thinking that underpins it.

❖ ❖ ❖

The rise of right-wing populism has also precipitated the blurring of boundaries between the far right and the mainstream – a process the author David Renton calls "convergence". In some countries, such as the US, populists have co-opted mainstream parties; in others, for example Italy, parties of the centre have formed governing coalitions with populists; and in others still, such as the UK, mainstream conservatives have taken on an increasingly populist tone in order to consolidate their voter base.

One result of this process is that conspiracist themes that circulate on the far right are aired more frequently in mainstream debate. In the UK, the Conservative MP Suella Braverman – now attorney general – was criticised by Jewish groups for her use of the phrase "cultural Marxism" at a public meeting in 2019. The year before, the right-wing *Daily Telegraph* ran a front-page story that accused George Soros of "backing [a] secret plot to stop Brexit". And notoriously, Theresa May's "citizens of nowhere" speech, delivered at the 2016 Conservative Party conference when she was prime minister, was criticised by some for echoing the antisemitic stereotype of rootless cosmopolitans.

This does not mean that every such utterance indicates hidden antisemitic beliefs: rather, that the encroachment of far-right politics on the mainstream has fostered a political style in which certain coded forms of antisemitism can flourish. Beyond the formal political space of elections and parties, the far right has carved out considerable space online in which populist themes can mix with more openly antisemitic content. The global far-right media platform

Breitbart frequently publishes content that repeats conspiracist themes – its founder, Andrew Breitbart, who was himself of Jewish background, was a key populariser of the "cultural Marxism" meme, for instance – but presents them in a way that gives them wider mainstream acceptability.

Jewish communities will always be threatened when these political currents thrive. Populist victories energise the wider far right, and antisemitic violence is one result: far-right terrorist attacks, including on Jewish places of worship in Europe and the US, have risen sharply in the last decade. What's more, Trump has now given us a lesson in how violent fascists can be directly mobilised to shore up support when a populist electoral project falters.

But the common language of the far right – the claim of an existential threat to the nation – is inherently destructive, even when Jews are not the main targets. In a brilliant reflection on the causes of the Holocaust, the late historian Moishe Postone argued that the Nazis were driven by a specifically modern form of antisemitism, one that offered a solution to the turbulence of crisis-ridden European capitalism. Its seductive promise was that order and coherence could be restored by turning abstract forces into an enemy with a name and a face, and then erasing it.

Across a turbulent world today, the far right is once again looking for an enemy to name. Adherents of Hindutva, the Hindu nationalist ideology that is currently tightening its grip over India, have perhaps the most revealing label for this enemy: the "anti-national". This menacing insult, thrown at government critics, religious minorities, and anyone else who refuses to conform to their straitjacket definition of belonging, is also a statement of intent. The history of Europe's Jews warns us of its ultimate possible conclusion – and our challenge today is to defend the people who fall into its path, and to dismantle the thinking that enables it.

THE ASHES ARE STILL WARM

Olga Grjasnowa

Translated by Katy Derbyshire

WHEN MY DAUGHTER was four, she went to a friend's house, where someone read to her from a children's book about Anne Frank. My daughter, named after her great-grandmother, a Holocaust survivor, knew nothing about Anne Frank or the Shoah until then. I had hoped it would stay that way a while longer. The children's book came abruptly and far too soon; it was oversimplified and problematically didactic. My daughter couldn't understand the Adolf Hitler "thing" either. She told me the content of the book very loudly on the bus home. What she said was right in principle, except she was convinced it was a book by Adolf Hitler.

German–Jewish relations are not the simplest. I live in a country that once declared the extermination of all Jewish life its official goal, and moved heaven and earth to achieve it. I live as a Jew in a country responsible for the Shoah and I live here among people who condoned that at the time and were perpetrators. There are still people here who sympathise with Nazi ideology, and there are more of them each day. I also write in a language that was the language of those perpetrators.

My relationship to the country is not exactly a love story. I emigrated from Azerbaijan to Germany with my parents and brother in 1996; we were what was called "quota refugees". None of us wanted to move to Germany; my mother, the daughter of a Shoah survivor, said at the time, "The ashes are still warm." But as holders of Azerbaijani passports, we had limited opportunities – and Germany was at least in Europe. There was no war raging here and my brother and I would have better chances, my parents hoped. I stayed in Germany, even though I fantasise at regular intervals about leaving the country again. But where would I go?

I have not solved that dilemma. My children were born in Germany and are growing up here, yet I find it hard to imagine they too will spend their lives here. This ambivalence towards Germany permeates my entire life. I am raising my children multilingually; not so they will have better career opportunities or for identity reasons, but because I don't trust this country. It is not only anti-semitism that worries me in Germany, but also racism.

Both take the form not only of verbal violence, but also of murders and terrorist attacks. Between 2000 and 2006, the National Socialist Underground (NSU), a far-right neo-Nazi terrorist group, carried out a series of murders in German cities. Ten people died. The police did not solve the murders but looked for the killers among the victims' acquaintances, while the media downplayed the racist killings as "kebab murders". The term, itself extremely racist, came about because two of the murder victims worked in a kebab shop. It was thought up by the *Nürnberger Zeitung*, a local newspaper that actually planned to write about a murder in a kebab shop but opted for "kebab murders" for layout reasons: with the result that people were compared to meat on spits, murdered German citizens were dehumanised even after their death. The German media continued to use the term for many years.

The NSU unmasked itself on 4 November 2011. Shortly afterwards, large numbers of files relating to the NSU were shredded, while the Hesse Office for the Protection of the Constitution has blocked access to many surviving files for 120 years. On 2 June 2019, Walter Lübke, the head of the Kassel municipal government, was murdered. He had spoken in favour of humanitarian treatment for refugees. In 2019, on 9 October, the day of Yom Kippur, an extreme right-wing terrorist attempted to attack the synagogue in Halle. He was armed; the only thing that protected the congregation from his Molotov cocktails and hand grenades was a wooden door. A large part was also played by the cantor, who noticed the man approaching. There were

51 people in the synagogue. It took the police around 20 minutes to reach the scene. Having failed to get into the synagogue, the man shot a passer-by dead and then drove to a kebab shop, where he also shot at guests and staff. On 19 February 2020, a right-wing radical murdered ten people in Hanau. His motive too was racism. On 4 October 2020, a man wearing a Bundeswehr (German army) uniform attacked a student outside a Hamburg synagogue, injuring him severely.

The following events took place less recently. On 9 November 1969, an assassination attempt was made on the chairman of the Central Council of Jews in Germany, Heinz Galinski. A bomb was planted in the Jewish Community Centre but did not go off. Galinski was in the room, along with 250 other people. A small radical left-wing group was responsible for the plot. On 13 February 1970, there was an attack on the Jewish community's retirement home in Munich. Seven people died, all of them survivors of National Socialism; two of them – David Jakubovicz and Eliakim Georg Pfau – had survived the German extermination camps. Here too, no one was ever held responsible. The chairman of the Jewish community said: "What could not be completed in the gas chambers has been accomplished 25 years later in a retirement home." On 26 October 1980, another right-wing extremist attack occurred at the Munich Oktoberfest. Twelve people were murdered, 221 injured. Although there were numerous leads to accomplices, none were ever found. The myth of the lone-wolf perpetrator prevailed. In the same year, Shlomo Levin, a publisher, and his partner Frida Poeschke were murdered by an antisemite. On 27 July 2000, a bomb was detonated at a commuter station in Düsseldorf. Ten people sustained life-threatening injuries, all of them immigrants from eastern Europe, six of them Jewish, and all of them on the way back from their German language course. No perpetrator was ever found, although there was very clear evidence of links to a known right-wing extremist.

It is important to detail all these attacks to emphasise that they were not isolated crimes, as the German government is so fond of suggesting. After the attack in Halle, the interior minister of Saxony-Anhalt still referred with utter conviction to an "irrational deed by a lone individual". There is a system behind it, as well as the constant downplaying of racism and antisemitism. The chronicle of these attacks in Ronen Steinke's book *Terror gegen Juden* (Terror against Jews) is 89 pages long, in small type. Of course, racism also plays a role among the left and in the whole of German society.

During the coronavirus pandemic, it became clear how quickly and effectively the German state can operate, with what urgency it can initiate and introduce changes – if it wishes to do so. The state investigated the left-wing Red Army Faction without mercy, while right-wing extremists are still classed as "isolated cases". There is no need to take isolated cases seriously; they can happen at any time and there is no way to prevent them.

In Germany, people like to pretend antisemitism stopped on 7 May 1945, as if no one in the country were antisemitic, and if they were, then it was the "Muslim" immigrants who brought antisemitism along with them. Philipp Amthor, an MP for the Christian Democratic Party (CDU), said exactly that in an interview with the news broadcaster n-tv, on the 75th anniversary of the liberation of Auschwitz extermination camp: "Antisemitism is particularly prevalent in Muslim-influenced cultural environments, of course. Bearing in mind the recent migration, there are, of course, many concerns on this front for the Jewish population." This narrative is relatively new.

There is no doubt that antisemitism also exists among Muslim immigrants; however, it is not related to their ethnic origins, as is often suggested in Germany, as though there were a genetic disposition towards antisemitism. While antisemitic crimes, such as attacks on synagogues, have repeatedly been committed by radical Islamists, most in Germany are committed by Germans on the far right. The numbers are clear, at least on the basis of hate crimes statistics for 2019: six crimes attributed to "left-wing" perpetrators, none of them violent, 57 crimes classed under "foreign ideologies", six of them violent, 24 antisemitic crimes under "religious ideologies", three of them violent, and a full 1,898 antisemitic crimes committed by right-wingers, including 62 acts of violence. Muslim antisemitism falls under the category of "religious ideologies". As recently as 2015, the then German interior minister Thomas de Maizière stated that radical Islamist antisemitism was the greatest threat and had to be paid particular heed. At the time, police attributed 80 per cent of that year's 1,596 antisemitic crimes to the right-wing spectrum. In his speech, de Maizière spoke almost exclusively about Islamism. It is obviously very important to take violent Islamist fundamentalism seriously, but what about the remaining 80 per cent? Why did he not take the right wing just as seriously as the Islamists?

The CDU politician Philipp Amthor was not the first person to draw on the myth of a "Judaeo-Christian" culture that had to be defended against Islam. Antisemitism is not in fact relevant in this debate. "Judeo-Christian" culture is constantly invoked by people positioning themselves against immigration. In all other cases, the phrase most commonly used is the "Christian Occident". The former president of the European Jewish Congress Michel Friedmann said in an interview with *Die Zeit*: "When people refer to this myth, I answer: you're so right, Jews and Christians have been living together for 2,000 years. The only problem is that Christians have been discriminating against Jews for 2,000 years and going on killing them at regular intervals."

Yet the myth seems to reposition the entire discourse. The question of German guilt appears to be solved, in one fell swoop. More than that, the suggestion is that German culture is in a position to protect Jews from antisemitism – even if that comes at the cost of the right to asylum. My family ended up in a Belarusian mass grave because the extermination of the Jews was the foremost goal of what was then mainstream German culture; my grandmother escaped because she found refuge in a "Muslim-influenced cultural environment" in Azerbaijan. That was where she met my grandfather, whose family had escaped the anti-Jewish pogroms in the Russian Pale of Settlement and found refuge from antisemitism in that very same Muslim-influenced cultural environment. The reinterpretation of the relationship between Christianity and Judaism is not only – to put it mildly – forgetful of history, but also a perfidious way to play off two minorities against each other, "the Jews" against "the Muslims", without ever addressing antisemitism or racism.

German commemorative culture is in a similar position. The Holocaust is frequently recalled and is taught in schools, yet knowledge of the structures and mechanisms of antisemitism, racism and the mass extermination of the Jews is barely existent. A 2019 study by the World Jewish Congress questioned 1,300 German men and women: 41 per cent of them expressed the opinion that Jews talked too much about the Holocaust. Views such as Jews holding too much power in the economy or bearing responsibility for most wars in the world also garnered relatively high approval levels. Almost half (48 per cent) were of the opinion that Jews are more loyal to Israel than to Germany. That sits well with the statement of the former head of the AFD (a fascistic party currently represented in the Bundestag), Alexander Gauland, in June 2018: "Hitler and the Nazis are nothing but a speck of bird shit in over a thousand years of successful German history."

❖ ❖ ❖

In my first 14 years in Germany, I had the feeling that, although antisemitism was always there, it was hidden – at least in public. Jokes about Jews were told in hushed tones. There was still a certain consensus about what could be said in public and what was not appropriate. That did not apply to racism more broadly. The atmosphere then shifted radically when the Social Democrat politician Thilo Sarazzin published his 2010 book *Deutschland schafft sich ab* (Germany is abolishing itself). Sarazzin spread racist theories, for instance pontifications on the "intelligence" of specific groups of immigrants, and sold several million copies of his book. After that, the spell was broken. People said loudly and vehemently what they had long been thinking. No one needs to hide their resentments these days.

In high culture too, antisemitism was just as present as in the rest of German society, for example, Günter Grass's antisemitic poem "Was gesagt werden muss" (What has to be said) in 2012, Martin Walser's controversial 1998 acceptance speech for the German Book Trade's Peace Prize, in which he spoke of the "moral cudgel of Auschwitz", or his 2002 novel *Tod eines Kritikers* (Death of a critic). The *FAZ* newspaper refused to print an advance extract from the novel and wrote, in an open letter to Walser, that the novel was "a document of hate" and "full of antisemitic clichés". Common to all these works is that the German public sphere showed some encouragement, but mainly objection.

There was the same critical response when Takis Würger brought out his novel *Stella* with the Hanser publishing house in 2019. The novel tells the story of the Jewish Gestapo collaborator Stella, based on the true story of Stella Goldschlag. It follows the unbroken narrative of the "beautiful Jewess" and centres on the question of Jewish culpability in the Shoah. It was thanks to this book that I understood how National Socialism could win over so many people – the author describes National Socialism in such naïve terms that I hoped it wasn't a calculated strategy. Presumably, however, that was not the author's intention. Yet all these incidents were accompanied by debate. Neither *Stella* nor *Tod eines Kritikers* was waved through without challenge or contradiction.

In 2020, the situation changed. Lisa Eckhart, a fictional character created by the Austrian comedian Lisa Lasselberger, had made a memorable appearance on German television in 2018. In a midnight cabaret show, she talked about the #metoo movement and named Harvey Weinstein, Roman Polanski and Woody Allen, asking whether "we can still watch their films with a clear conscience now that we know that all three of them are..." There follows a pause for effect so that the audience can fill in the blank for themselves, and Eckhart continues after a brief shudder: "Oh, I don't want to say it. And as if that wasn't bad enough, now they've also been abusing women." As if what wasn't bad enough? They being Jews? Eckhart goes on, to make sure no one misses the point, saying their names again, making it clear that Allen was born Allen-Königsberg. Now she says: "Don't you think this 'metoo' thing is antisemitic?" The first laughs from the audience. "But it's all well and good that we're now allowing the Jews to attack a few women. We can't make up for anything with money. I mean, paying reparations to the Jews is like treating Didi Mateschitz to a Red Bull." She follows up with comments about people of colour, people with disabilities and political correctness. Then she returns to the Jews: "But we're most disappointed with the Jews, we've always been railing against the stupid accusation that they only care about money, and all of a sudden it turns out they really don't care about money, they care about women, and that's why they need the money. We've finally freed our wards from the clutches of the right wing and then they do something like this."

That was not an isolated case. During another appearance on the same channel, she said: "I spent three years in Paris as a student of German literature. Studying German literature here wasn't embarrassing enough for me. But no, the truth is, I wanted to be seen as a linguistic wunderkind over there, so I pretended to be Polish. They found me out though and they said: it's very simple – you can study German as a foreign language. And in the end, I was teased even more than a Jew taking business studies." Roars of laughter.

Two years later, Lisa Eckhart was scheduled to read from her debut novel at a literary festival in Hamburg. Her appearance was cancelled due to alleged threats from the left, which soon proved to be false. It was then claimed that two writers had refused to share a stage with her. One of them, Benjamin Quaderer, clarified that he had pulled out of the event but not demanded that Lisa Eckhart should be uninvited. Eckhart's novel, incidentally, is about her grandmother in 1945 and is nourished by the same resentments as her comedy routine.

I have watched that TV appearance on WDR's *Mitternachtsspitzen* several times, and I still don't know how anyone could think her statements were not antisemitic. One can of course claim that the artist is free to unmask clichés; except that is exactly what she doesn't do. She lets everything stand without comment and grants the audience its guffaws. However the Federal Association of Departments for Research and Information on Antisemitism (RIAS) criticised the routine: "Lisa Eckhart does not make jokes about antisemitism or antisemites in her piece; instead, she reproduces antisemitic, racist, sexist and ableist stereotypes. These stereotypes are not ironically refracted in any way; the comedy is supposed to arise from the alleged violation of taboos." Criticism also came from the American Jewish Committee (AJC) Berlin and the German government's antisemitism commissioner, Felix Klein.

However something remarkable has taken place in the German public sphere. The German branch of PEN leapt to Lisa Eckhart's defence, and even Navid Kermani, another holder of the German Books Trade's Peace Prize and an author I respect very highly, gave a speech upholding freedom of speech and complaining that Eckhart had been made "contemptible". The journalist Sebastian Hammelehle wrote in *Der Spiegel* about "ambiguity". Are

Eckhart's statements ambiguous? On a German cultural magazine programme, she was asked: "Are we allowed to make fun of Jews?" and "What is satire allowed to do nowadays?" As if that was what this was about. Eckhart propagates antisemitic prejudices, which are not dissected. Her audience laughs not at a good punchline but about Jews, while she stands alongside and bathes in that laughter. She consciously oversteps boundaries, without any power relations being questioned or knowledge being gained, except perhaps that the Germans still really like laughing at jokes about Jews. In her recent show *Die Vorteile des Lasters* she was asking: "Wieso sind in Sachen Humor die Juden den Frauen zwei Nasenlängen voraus?" and referred to the stereotype of the hooked "Jewish nose."

When interviewed, Eckhart said that her critics lacked goodwill. Eckhart defended herself on Austrian television: "All members of the Jewish community allegedly feel attacked by it? I have to say, that's accusing Jews of humourlessness, which verges on antisemitism." Earnest consideration of an antisemitism accusation would sound very different. Then again, her book is selling like hot cakes and the antisemitism may have fulfilled its purpose: PR.

I am honestly appalled at how much benevolence Eckhart has received. Especially as there was another debate a few months before the Eckhart incident, in this case about Achille Mbembe. The historian was invited to give the opening speech at the Ruhr Triennial. Then, however, he was accused of antisemitism. A passage from Mbembe's work was cited to claim that he had compared the Holocaust to apartheid, thus relativising the Holocaust. He was also accused of comparing the Israeli state with apartheid South Africa and thereby disputing Israel's right to exist. The German government's antisemitism commissioner Felix Klein spoke out against Mbembe. Here is the passage in question: "The apartheid system in South Africa and the destruction of Jews in Europe – the latter, though, in an extreme fashion and within a quite different setting – constituted two emblematic manifestations of this fantasy of separation." Mbembe did not give his speech and was subjected to systematic public discreditation. Neither German PEN nor Kermani stood up for Mbembe. When it comes to deciding whether statements are antisemitic in Germany, it seems to make a difference who makes them. Just as blaming Muslims for the rise in antisemitism absolves Germany of its guilt, selective recognition of antisemitism when it comes to public figures also neatly removes the responsibility of acknowledging racism against Jews as a German problem.

German society is currently discussing police violence; a new "isolated case" comes to light every day. Group chats in which police officers share pictures of Hitler and horrific racist and antisemitic statements, in some cases even while guarding a synagogue. Police officers calling up the data of people they disagree with on police computers. Police officers collecting Nazi paraphernalia and stockpiling weapons. Interior Minister Horst Seehofer refusing to allow an investigation into racism in the police force.

The problem also exists in the German army, incidentally, where "isolated" extreme right-wing soldiers keep coming to our attention – for instance an entire underground network that was planning a coup or a soldier who hid a gun in a toilet at Vienna airport and also posed successfully as a Syrian refugee. The situation in Germany is not getting easier, but at least we now know what we are dealing with. Whether that's any consolation, I cannot say.

BLOODY JEWS

Jo Glanville

AT EASTER WEEKEND, in a wood outside Norwich, England, a forester finds the body of a boy. There are signs that the child has been tortured. The forester swiftly concludes from the nature of the wounds that the local Jews are guilty of the murder: no Christian would have committed such a crime. Word gets around the city, people begin gathering on the streets and an accusation against the local Jews starts spreading. The body becomes something of a ghoulish attraction as crowds of visitors go to look at it over the weekend. The child is identified as William, a 12-year-old apprentice tanner whose workmanship was actually popular with the Jews. The story of his killing in 12th-century East Anglia is the first recorded case of an accusation of ritual murder against a Jewish community. It is also one of the first claims of a Jewish conspiracy in Christian Europe. The allegation would be repeated across England and Europe, migrate to the Middle East in the 19th century, lead to new accusations in the 20th century and continue to surface today.

On 27 April 2019, an open letter was posted on the online forum 8chan. It was written in the name of John T Earnest, who murdered a 60-year-old woman and injured three other people, including the rabbi, when he opened fire that day at a synagogue in Poway, San Diego. In an antisemitic rant of more than 4,000 words, the letter warned of the genocide being planned by Jews and recycled multiple conspiracy theories, including control of the media, usury, cultural Marxism and ritual murder. It emotively addressed the alleged victim of a murder in the 15th century as if he were a recent casualty: "You are not forgotten Simon of Trent, the horror that you and countless children have endured at the hands of the Jews will never be forgiven." Simon of Trent is one of the most notorious ritual-murder accusations, a "blood libel". Members of the Jewish community in Trent, Italy, were accused of killing a toddler and using his blood for ritual purposes. Thirteen Jews were executed, after protracted interrogation and torture. The pope launched an investigation into the case, issuing a papal bull that prohibited violence against Jews. However this did not have much effect in the long term: there were 26 cases in the 16th century (Luther also helped to stoke the belief in the ritual-murder charge) and a revival of allegations in the 19th and early 20th century.

How does a medieval libel still have such cultural resonance and appeal? It comes from another time and place, when mistrust and prejudice against Jews was based on the Jewish religion rather than race, and Jews were one of the few minorities in Europe. It plays on a fundamental communal fear – the kidnap of children by outsiders. It is also gory and pornographic, which always appeals to an audience. And it preserves the idea of Jews as satanic plotters, which has underpinned conspiracy theories about them ever since. From the first claim of ritual murder in 12th-century England, it has been recycled by the most celebrated authors (from Chaucer to Shakespeare and Dickens) as well as in popular literature, handed down as a horror story that has been cited as proof, over and over, of Jewish iniquity. The lawyer and writer Anthony Julius has called it the "ur-story" of English literary antisemitism.

In the most detailed account of the first allegation of ritual murder in 1144, the author, a monk in Norwich Cathedral priory called Thomas of Monmouth, produced evidence that it was a Jewish plot. He quoted the chilling testimony of a Jewish convert, a fellow monk called Theobald, who told Thomas that the Jews could not win their freedom or "ever return to the lands of their fathers" unless they shed human blood. Thomas's source revealed that the leaders of the Jews in Spain gathered annually to cast lots and select a region where a Christian would be sacrificed. That year, "the lot fell on the men of Norwich", and the Jews across England agreed for the murder to take place there.

Here are the ingredients that would come to be recycled repeatedly in the narrative of the Jewish conspiracy: Jews gathering together in a secret meeting; Jews malevolently plotting to cause harm; Jews acting in a network with international reach; Jews endowed with magical powers. It is astonishing not only that the template of the Jewish plot was formed so early, but that its elements have changed so little over nearly 900 years. The perception of Jews as a globally united group, operating clandestinely across borders, has survived as a formula to be applied in any era, and Thomas of Monmouth's account has continued to be cited as evidence by antisemites. The British fascist Arnold Leese, who was prosecuted in 1936 for accusing Jews of ritual murder, published a pamphlet after his release from prison and listed Thomas of Monmouth's witness Theobald in a list of Jewish converts from 1144 to 1913 who gave evidence of ritual murder. Leese's writing is still circulating in American neo-Nazi groups. Reviewing the origins of these accusations provides some clues to their durability. It reveals not only how early stories of conspiracy became embedded in European popular culture, but also that the motives for casting the Jews as plotters and murderers were often political. Demonising Jews could be profitable.

When William's body was found in the wood, it is thought that the local Jews had been living in Norwich for just a decade, after first arriving in England less than a hundred years previously with William the Conqueror. As newcomers, outsiders and foreigners, they may have been regarded with suspicion, but they also arrived with a backstory that Thomas of Monmouth exploited to the full: the Jews of Norwich do not just kill William, they crucify him. "This link between Jews past and Jews present had never before been so boldly attempted," the historian Miri Rubin observes. "[Thomas] remade Christian history in a contemporary English city." In their bloodthirsty murder of the child, William's Jewish killers "could not extinguish their mad cruelty, nor satisfy their inborn hatred of the Christian name": they want revenge on Jesus, whom they blame for their exile. "Just as we have condemned Christ to a most shameful death, so we condemn a Christian... that which they ascribe to us we will inflict on them." In 12th-century Norwich, Thomas was keen to demonstrate that the local Jews had form: they were as dangerous and vindictive as their ancestors in the New Testament. These were long-term enemies.

❖ ❖ ❖

The betrayal of Jesus is the prototype of the Jewish conspiracy. In the Gospel of Matthew, the chief priests, the scribes and the elders meet at the palace of the high priest to plot to kill Jesus. In the Gospel of Luke, they meet with Judas to hatch the plan. Although the Romans executed Jesus, it is the Jewish people who insistently call for his crucifixion when Pilate offers to release him. The Jews, as Jesus's disciples, were as much his friends as his enemies, but it is the story of the betrayal that has defined their role in the Christian narrative. In the early history of Christianity, the writers of the New Testament and the theologians who came after had their own polemical motives for damning the Jews as they laid the foundations for a new religion and sought to make sense of its relationship with its Jewish origins. What started as a theological rift between a new Jewish sect that recognised Jesus as the Messiah and the Jews who rejected him became central to the Christian story and shaped the perception of the Jewish people. It is probably the longest-lasting group character assassination in history, and the ritual murder accusation revived the smear. By replaying the crucifixion, Thomas of Monmouth was reaffirming the original sin of the Jews: this was not a random murder; it was a re-enactment of a theological drama. The Jews as a group were guilty once again: the people of Norwich would not be satisfied with punishing the perpetrators; they chillingly called for the destruction of "all the Jews... root and branch".

Thomas of Monmouth has been credited with inventing the ritual-murder charge. If Christianity laid the foundation for the reputation of Jews as conspirators, then Thomas may have been among the first to kick off the modern version of an ancient narrative. The many accusations of ritual murder that followed William of Norwich, elsewhere in England and later across Europe, inspired poems, ballads, plays, pamphlets and broadsheets. The *Nuremberg Chronicle*, published in 1493, retold the stories of William of Norwich and Simon of Trent, with bloodthirsty woodcut illustrations; pirated editions later appeared across

Europe, from Budapest to Paris. Single-page broadsheets with poems and images of ritual murder would be used as prompts for storytelling. These horror stories are perhaps the tributaries of modern antisemitism, entering the stream of cultural life as macabre popular entertainment and resurfacing as Shylock with his demand for Christian blood and later as vampires, whose bloodsucking diet and hooked noses recast the medieval fear of Jews in Gothic clothing. The QAnon conspiracy theory, now circulating in the mainstream, claimed that children were murdered for their blood as part of a fiendish plot against President Trump, and is perhaps the most recent recycling of the myth. The consumption of blood is in fact prohibited in Judaism.

A folk song inspired by a ritual-murder accusation in Lincoln in 1255, more than a century after events in Norwich, has entered the canon of English folk music. The story of the killing of an eight-year-old child called Hugh in Lincoln followed the same pattern as that of William in Norwich. This time, however, there were more serious consequences for the Jewish community. Once again it was a conspiracy, only on this occasion all the Jews of England were implicated: "[the Jews of Lincoln] sent to almost all the cities of England where the Jews lived, and summoned some of their sect from each city to be present at a sacrifice to take place at Lincoln," wrote the chronicler Matthew Paris. Once again the child was crucified, as a deliberate insult to Christ. This time it was a more detailed, even gorier re-enactment of the crucifixion, with one Jew taking the role of Pilate and the rest replaying the humiliation of Christ. Ninety-one Jews were arrested and 18 were hanged in London.

The folk song inspired by the killing, "Sir Hugh, or, the Jew's Daughter", has had a remarkably long life, much to the shame of at least one contemporary folk historian. "I am at a loss to understand why revivalist singers keep on singing it," wrote Vic Gammon in the sleeve notes to a reissue of the folk singer AL Lloyd's rendition in 2011. The story, Gammon noted, had led to the death of innocent people, though as a ballad he rated it as one of the best of its kind. In the most common version of the song, Hugh is playing ball with his friends. The ball goes through the window of the Jew's house and his daughter invites Hugh inside, enticing him with an apple. She then murders him with a penknife. Hugh's mother comes searching for him, and the dead boy eerily calls to her, enabling her to find him. The conspiracy and crucifixion do not feature in this version of the song, but traces of the ritual murder remain in a number of others: the Jew's daughter collects the boy's blood. "She set him in a golden chair,/ and jaggd [sic] him with a pin,/And called for a goolden [sic] cup/To houl his heart's blood in."

The American scholar Francis James Child, a pioneering 19th-century archivist and historian of English folk music, included 18 different versions of the song in his multi-volume history. They came from Northamptonshire, Shropshire, Buckinghamshire and London, as well as Scotland, Ireland, New York and Baltimore. It's remarkable evidence of how far a story can travel across regions, continents and centuries through folk music, partly thanks to migration. The historian William Wells Newell, a contemporary of Child's, wrote that he heard a group of African-American children in New York singing a version of the song, then traced the source to a little girl, whose mother's parents were Irish. The family was perilously squatting in a hut on a construction site where brownstones were being built near Central Park. Newell paints a remarkable picture of extreme poverty in 19th-century New York in his dogged quest for original folk music: rocks from controlled explosions flew over the roof of the hut, which was perched on a rock, and clouds of dust blew into the family home, "an unswept hovel". All references to Jews had disappeared from this version and the Jew's daughter had become a duke's daughter: it had been neutralised, but other versions still circulated in America with the original cast of characters. The British folk archivist Cecil Sharp collected nine versions of the song in the remote southern Appalachian mountains during the First World War.

The survival of "Sir Hugh" (Steeleye Span recorded a jolly rendition in 1975, stripped of Jewish references; Sam Lee recorded a haunting version in 2012) is an outstanding example of how the fantasy of Jewish malevolence can endure in popular culture. Just the tail remains of the original story, and few people who sing the song now may be aware of its history, but it is perhaps this very dislocation that has helped to entrench antisemitism. The roots are no longer visible, but the image of Jews as dangerous lives on, passed down through the centuries in something as apparently benign as a folk song.

As Child was publishing his monumental history of folk songs in the late 19th century, there was a revival in accusations of ritual murder. He made an enlightened rebuttal of the allegations in his essay on the song, at a time when others were actually giving the charge credibility: "These pretended child-murders, with their horrible consequences, are only a part of a persecution which, with all moderation, may be rubricated as the most disgraceful chapter in the history of the human race." Child cited a case in Tisza-Eszlar, Hungary, the year that the first volume of his collection of folk songs was published in 1882, when 15 Jews were arrested and imprisoned for a year before their release, as well as others in Russia, Germany, Rhodes, Alexandria and Wallachia (current day Romania).

This revival of the original conspiracy theory coincided with the birth of antisemitism as a political movement in the late 19th century in Germany and Austria. The emergence of a new racist ideology absorbed the long established demonising narrative: the old tropes helped to stoke the new rhetoric. Between 1867 and 1914, there were 12 ritual-murder trials. One resulted in a conviction – for murder, not for ritual murder. The antisemitic publication *Der Stürmer* repeatedly recycled ritual-murder accusations in the 1920s and 1930s. Its publisher, Julius Streicher, was prosecuted on more than one occasion for claiming that child murders or disappearances were Jewish ritual killings. Heinrich Himmler, head of the SS, cynically proposed faking accusations of ritual murder for the purpose of antisemitic propaganda. In 1943, he wrote to the Reich's security chief, Ernst Kaltenbrunner, suggesting that the security police should seek out reports of missing children "so that we can repeat in our radio broadcasts to England that in the town of XY a child is missing and that it is probably another case of ritual murder".

This naked opportunism has frequently been core to the charge of ritual murder: accusing Jews of fantastic crimes has often served a political purpose. When the Jews were expelled from the royal domain in France in 1182, ritual murder was one of the pretexts for their expulsion. The king seized all their property. This included Jewish buildings and land in Paris, where the king subsequently built the market les Halles. The historian EM Rose has stated that this expropriation of Jewish wealth "underwrote the very fabric of the city", including the paving of the roads, the building of the city walls and the founding of the university. The ritual-murder charge was a "tool" for extorting money.

❖ ❖ ❖

When the British fascist Arnold Leese wrote his pamphlet *My Irrelevant Defence* in 1938, an attempt to prove his claims about ritual murder, the Nazis were already recycling the allegation as part of antisemitic propaganda. *Der Stürmer* published a special issue on ritual murder in 1934. Leese described the publisher of *Der Stürmer*, Julius Streicher, who was executed at Nuremberg, as "a gallant and faithful German officer", not the "crazy and sadistic devil" he was made out to be. Leese's organisation, the Imperial Fascist League, had a negligible membership, but his own influence on the next generation of fascists was notable. Colin Jordan, who went on to found the BNP with John Tyndall, was a follower. After Leese's death, his home in Princedale Road, west London, became the BNP headquarters. Antisemitic conspiracy theories remained central to the ideology of both Jordan and Tyndall.

The discovery of the Jewish conspiracy was the moment of conversion for Leese. It's a disturbingly common theme in the life story of a number of British fascists: suddenly the world makes sense to them. The turning point came when Leese was given a copy of *The Protocols of the Elders of Zion*, the notorious forgery that claimed to be the minutes from a meeting in which the Jews detailed their plans for world domination: "Everything in this little book rang true." Leese believed that Jews had covered up the ritual-murder story and that this was proof of "Jewish Money Power's" domination, his unwieldy term for the Jewish conspiracy, capitalised to elevate it to a bogus category.

Perhaps part of the continuing appeal of the ritual-murder conspiracy to fascists like Leese and neo-Nazis today is that it appears to offer evidence of Jewish evil. The historian Ronnie Po-chia Hsia has credited the myth of child murders in the Middle Ages with "creating a knowledge to be transmitted under the guise of history". There is literature to point to, cases to refer to and even trials, amounting to some kind of "proof". From Thomas of Monmouth's account to a trial for ritual murder in Kiev in 1913, there was a catalogue of alleged crimes to reference. The claims of conspiracy had been repeated so often, the pattern of the murders and accusations was so similar, that they must be true.

Eleven days before John T Earnest attacked the synagogue in San Diego in April 2019, the American neo-Nazi Andrew Anglin posted an essay about ritual murder on his website the Daily Stormer (named after Julius Streicher's publication *Der Stürmer*). There is no evidence at the time of writing to suggest that the post had a direct influence on Earnest, but it indicates the neo-Nazi culture to which he was exposed and how the conspiracy of ritual murder has become a fixture in its racist narrative. Anglin's site has influential international reach in fomenting anti-semitism: he orchestrated online abuse of the British politician Luciana Berger and personally encouraged followers to create multiple Twitter accounts to harass her in 2014. In July 2019, a US magistrate judge recommended that Anglin pay more than $14m in damages to a Jewish woman he had targeted in a campaign of harassment.

On his ritual-murder blog, Anglin posted a video of a Jewish woman in eastern Europe. In an English transcript, she is reported hectoring passengers on a bus and threatening to slaughter and crucify them in a synagogue. Anglin wrote that the woman was "clearly insane" and that her behaviour was not typical of "normal Jews", but that she was describing a Jewish practice: "ritual torture and murder, which we have known for a thousand years does indeed take place inside of their synagogues". The post included some of the most gory medieval illustrations of children being murdered by groups of Jews, including one of Simon of Trent, the 15th-century ritual-murder case that Earnest referred to in his letter in his catalogue of Jewish conspiracies. It is an engraving from the *Nuremberg Chronicle*, the 15th-century book that helped to spread the ritual-murder accusation across Europe, showing the child being horribly tortured as Jews collect his blood in a bowl. "The bottom line that you need to understand is that the Jews are literally a satanic force," wrote Anglin, "and it is satan [sic] that drives them. They are inhuman, monstrous creatures which as a point of fact and of general principle absolutely must be completely exterminated if goodness, godliness and anything true is to continue to exist in the world of men." There is a disclaimer on the Daily Stormer website that states: "We here at the Daily Stormer are opposed to violence. We seek revolution through the education of the masses." Anyone who suggests or promotes violence in the comments section will be banned. This does not, apparently, apply to Anglin's own incitement to murder Jews. A comment in response to Anglin's post recommended Arnold Leese's pamphlet on ritual murder ("another good free book on jew [sic] ritual murder"). This marginal English fascist's writing has joined the neo-Nazi reading list, circulating with the medieval accounts in a perpetuating cycle of demonisation.

It is easy to spot the echoes of ritual murder in a cartoon of a grinning Israeli soldier with his mouth, teeth and hands covered in blood (shared on social media by a Labour Party member in the UK, a local councillor, in 2016). The hooked nose, the delight in killing and the suggestion of drinking blood are all stereotypes of European antisemitism, descendants of the caricatures in *Der Stürmer* and medieval illustrations of Jews murdering children. With their inclusion, no cartoon can claim to be a political commentary on the abuses of the Israeli state – it becomes a racist attack on all Jews. What emboldens the member of a mainstream political party to share an image like this? In this case, the politician apologised and claimed that he had not properly read "one content" [sic]. The Labour Party suspended the councillor and then reinstated him, with backbench responsibilities only. The local Labour group claimed that there was no evidence of similar previous conduct on social media. "Indeed there is evidence to the contrary. He is opposed to racism in all forms."

If you are opposed to racism, you cannot apparently be an antisemite, even if you have distributed antisemitic expression. It is a perplexing example of doublethink that is partly explained by the left's history of opposition to Zionism as a colonialist enterprise, which appeared to have blinded some party members to their support for antisemitic tropes. It is a blindness that also betrays a striking and perhaps wilful cultural amnesia: amnesia about the Holocaust, amnesia about the history of persecution that long predates the Holocaust and amnesia or perhaps ignorance about England's unique role in triggering the ritual-murder accusation and with it the longevity of the conspiracy theory. The association of Jews with blood, harm and conspiracy has entered so deeply into European and American culture that there no longer appears to be awareness of its origins or sensitivity to its toxic impact. It's time for some remembrance.

JEWS BEHAVING BADLY

Philip Spencer

THE RECENT EMERGENCE of antisemitism on the left is the latest version of a way of thinking about Jews that goes back to their emancipation more than 200 years ago, when they were given rights within western societies for the first time. The idea that the status of Jews in Europe was a problem requiring a solution, known as the "Jewish Question", began circulating as the left was emerging as a political force in the 18th century. Some supported Jewish emancipation at the time on consistently universalist grounds, believing that all human beings, regardless of their birth, ancestry or religion, were entitled to the same rights. But for others it was conditional on Jews behaving "well", and effectively ceasing to be Jews by assimilating fully into society, abandoning their religion (seen as peculiarly backward) and their overriding loyalty to each other (as it was perceived).

This conditional approach to emancipation was rooted in a particular and fundamentally flawed explanation of antisemitism: as an effect of Jews having been excluded from society and civilisation in the past. The ghettos in which Jews had been confined were seen as the fundamental cause of their supposedly "bad" behaviour, in which they dishonestly exaggerated their suffering, and engaged in special pleading for malign and purely self-interested reasons. The dangerous corollary of this explanation is that if Jews continued to behave "badly", then antisemitism might now be understandable, even condoned. It might be the case that Jews should be blamed if things did not work out the way the left imagined they should or would. Whilst the right would blame Jews for conditions deteriorating economically or politically after emancipation, some on the left saw Jews as an obstacle (perhaps even the major obstacle) to things changing for the better. Antisemitism might then make a kind of sense on the left as well as the right. It might even be part of a popular movement for change itself. (For the antisemitic right, Jews should never have been given rights because they had never belonged and could never belong.)

This viewpoint can be found among 19th-century anarchist thinkers such as Proudhon, Fourier and Bakunin, but also among some of Marx's successors, who thought there might be a progressive kernel in antisemitism. In the 20th century, some in the international communist movement argued that those who objected to Jewish capitalists might then be persuaded to object to capitalism *tout court*.

This perception of Jews standing in the way of progress played out in the long-running furore over antisemitism in the Labour Party under Jeremy Corbyn's leadership, which erupted following his election in 2015 and continued to divide the party even after his departure. Corbyn's supporters insisted that accusations of antisemitism were simply being "weaponised" to smear the party leader personally and to prevent the election of potentially the most radical Labour government ever. They argued that antisemitism was being wilfully and dishonestly confused with anti-Zionism, as a strategy supposedly adopted by Zionists to deflect and dismiss legitimate criticism of Israel. Anti-Zionism was, for them, a wholly legitimate position, one rightly taken by Corbyn for many years as a necessary part of his principled and fundamentally anti-racist opposition to western imperialism (Israel being seen as an outpost of colonialism).

Complaints that Corbyn had failed to tackle antisemitism within the party led to high-profile resignations and, in 2019, the Equalities and Human Rights Commission (EHRC) opened an investigation to determine whether the Labour Party had unlawfully discriminated against, harassed or victimised people because they are Jewish. Its findings, published in October 2020, revealed a sustained lack of leadership on the issue, significant failings in the way the party handled antisemitism complaints and a host of examples of harassment, discrimination and political interference. The party's conduct has had a profound impact on Jewish people, at variance with its stated commitment to a zero-tolerance approach to antisemitism. The only other party to have previously been referred to the EHRC was the far-right British National Party. The referral of the Labour Party was particularly serious, given the left's historic commitment to anti-racism and its understanding that racism can take place at an institutional and not just individual level. An important element of that understanding is the principle that the voices of those who feel they have experienced racism need in the first instance to be taken very seriously, which is precisely what many Jews felt strongly was not the case in the Labour Party.

As committed anti-racists (which is indeed why they were anti-Zionist), Corbyn's supporters could not possibly consider themselves antisemitic. In their view, antisemitism itself either does not exist at all or is wilfully exaggerated (in an echo of the attitude towards Jews who came out of the ghetto after emancipation). It may have been a problem in the past, but no longer. Other forms of racism by contrast are much more important, including against Britain's substantial Muslim population (in the form of Islamophobia) but also especially against Britain's Black population, where continuing racism is the poisonous legacy of imperialism and slavery.

Moreover, in sharp contrast to the real victims of racism, Jews are supposedly now so well integrated that they have become part of the global power structure. Within western societies they have supposedly even become "white", an argument that has been advanced especially in the United States by those who compare the fortunes of Jews after the Second World War with the continuing structural racism that derives from slavery. On this account, antisemitism has largely disappeared and Jews have become fully integrated into American society and are now indeed generally extremely successful, both economically and politically. Not only have Jews strongly supported the civil rights movement in the United States, which suggests that large numbers of Jews did not (and do not) see themselves as in any way defenders of a white power structure, but the argument at a theoretical level rests on what is, on closer inspection, an extremely problematic notion of "whiteness". It is not, moreover, a view, it has to be said, which is shared by the growing number of white supremacists who are still very keen on murdering Jews, as the Pittsburgh massacre showed in 2018.

In the contemporary world, the notion of Jews continuing to behave badly, and of antisemitism therefore somehow being understandable and even justified, has attached itself especially to Israel and to the large majority of Jews who support its continued existence. Israel is cast here as the worst state in the world, uniquely reactionary because it is (supposedly unlike any other state) based on ethnic criteria. It is a state which supposedly commits the most appalling crimes we know of – apartheid, crimes against humanity, even genocide. The latter charge is particularly and deliberately shocking since it turns the victims of the most radical genocide (to date) into today's perpetrators of the crime. Jews, on this account, have not only failed uniquely to learn the lessons of the Holocaust, they have themselves become the Nazis of today.

In continuing to moan about suffering from an antisemitism which no longer exists, they are apparently engaging in special pleading, attempting to advance their own selfish interests, acting once again in opposition to the interests of wider society, both in the UK and globally, and, worst of all, doing so to protect Israel from criticism. Furthermore, as part of the west, through Israel and the so-called "Zionist lobby", Jews play a key role in the imperialist subjugation of the rest of the world, even on some accounts organising it themselves (as in the idea that there was a Zionist conspiracy to persuade America to launch the Iraq war).

Conversely, all who oppose Israel's existence must, by definition, be seen as part of the forces of progress, as friends and allies. Those who begin by opposing Israel may then oppose the west more generally, since Israel is its tool (or vice versa). Antisemitism, once known as the "socialism of fools", has now effectively become what has been called the "anti-imperialism of fools".

What all of this amounts to is that Jews are once again being blamed by some on the left for behaving badly. All those who claim that antisemitism is real today must, by definition, be doing so dishonestly: trying to exploit their suffering (abusing the Holocaust); pretending they are still enduring antisemitism when they cannot be; engaging in special pleading for malign self-interested reasons, acting in league with (if not even organising) the forces of reaction, not just locally but globally.

This way of thinking underpinned a further key development in this unhappy saga: the reaction of Corbyn and his supporters in the summer of 2018 to the adoption of the International Holocaust Remembrance Alliance (IHRA) definition of antisemitism. The IHRA definition has been accepted by many governments. In the UK it has been adopted by the national government, the Scottish government, the Welsh Assembly, the Crown Prosecution Service, the National Union of Students and more than 260 local authorities, many Labour-held. The IHRA document states that antisemitism may be expressed as hatred toward Jews and then gives a series of examples which include but "are not limited to" the following: accusing the Jews as a people, or Israel as a state, of inventing or exaggerating the Holocaust; accusing Jewish citizens of being more loyal to Israel, or to the alleged priorities of Jews worldwide, than to the interests of their own nation; denying the Jewish people their right to self-determination, for example by claiming that the existence of a state of Israel is a racist endeavour; and drawing comparisons of contemporary Israeli policy to that of the Nazis. The document specifically states that "criticism of Israel similar to that levelled against any other country cannot be regarded as anti-Semitic". Under Corbyn, the Labour Party tried to rewrite the Israel-related points, and especially wanted to remove the charge that it is antisemitic to argue that a state of Israel is *per se* a racist endeavour. This was far more than an objection to the policies of any Israeli government at any moment in time. It was an objection to the idea that there should ever be such a state.

From this perspective, if there is any antisemitism now (when it is not being denied outright), it can only be because of Israel and thus effectively because of the way Jews themselves behave. Jews themselves are therefore responsible for antisemitism. If they did not continue to behave so badly, then there would be little or no antisemitism, in the UK or anywhere else in the modern world.

The Holocaust might have been expected to have put an end to any such temptations on the left. The Soviet Union, in fact, deliberately revived antisemitism after the catastrophe, at a time when it commanded the loyalty of many on the left, especially after its part in the defeat of Nazi Germany. While the Holocaust was taking place, and in parts of the Soviet Union occupied by the Nazis, the regime had systematically downplayed what was being done to the Jews. The figure of 33,771 Jews massacred at Babi Yar in Ukraine in 1941 was revised down to 1,000. This was compounded by a sustained policy afterwards of repressing any effort to memorialise and grieve over what had happened to Jews: to give only one example, the manuscript and entire edition of *The Black Book* by Ilya Ehrenburg and Vasily Grossman, documenting Nazi crimes against the Jewish people, was destroyed as part of the liquidation of the Jewish Anti-Fascist Committee. The trumped-up charges against the latter were in turn part of the Stalinist regime's development of its own unique form of antisemitism, attacking Jews for being simultaneously Zionist (so nationalist) and cosmopolitan (so anti-nationalist). This contradictory accusation relied on casting Jews as mortal enemies of progress and engaged in a conspiracy with the imperialist west. It was central to a whole set of purge trials that then rocked communist-controlled eastern Europe, especially the Slánský trial in Czechoslovakia in 1952, in which Jewish communists were forced to confess to a fabricated Zionist conspiracy.

The Soviet Union's legacy lives on in much of the anti-Zionism espoused by a part of the left today. It first promoted the idea that Israel was a tool of western imperialism in the Middle East and that Zionism was a form (the worst form moreover) of racism, abandoning its initial support for Israel once it became clear that the state would not take its side in the cold war.

But at another level, the Holocaust has even come to be used as a new way of attacking Jews themselves. Firstly, some on the left view the Holocaust as a case of general racism, not unique, but as just one example of what racists (especially in the west) have long practised. (Jeremy Corbyn's attempt, with other MPs, to rename Holocaust Memorial Day as Genocide Memorial Day in 2011 is one instance of this.) This perception understands racism itself in a very inadequate way, as an ideology which essentially casts its victims as inferior and less than human. Anti-semitism has always been more complex than this, because Jews were seen by the Nazis (and their predecessors) as not only inferior but also extremely powerful, engaged in a global conspiracy to control the world. Secondly, there is a perception that the Holocaust put an end to antisemitism (if only this were true). According to this view, if there is still any antisemitism, it only exists on the neo-Nazi far right, which denies the Holocaust, and is a marginal phenomenon. Antisemitism is confined to the past. If Jews now complain about an antisemitism which scarcely exists, they must be doing so once again for malign and self-interested reasons, placing their needs over and above those who do actually continue to suffer a real and much more serious racism.

❖ ❖ ❖

If we think about the antisemitism that has been a source of such debate and conflict on the left in the UK in recent years in this light, what we might see is less the emergence of a new phenomenon than its re-emergence in a new form. Antisemitism is not invariant or eternal, though it may sometimes seem so. Rather it has to be thought of as something that has taken various forms and shapes at different times since the emancipation that promised so much in the 18th and 19th centuries.

What has been continuous since then has been the idea held by some on the left that Jews have somehow failed to keep their side of the bargain. They have not abandoned their loyalty to each other (witness their support for Israel); they have continued to behave badly by complaining about antisemitism when it cannot (after the

Holocaust) any longer be significant today. Since emancipation, antisemitism has only been seen as significant in the past, and never the present. What is new is that this form of antisemitism today comes wrapped in the mantle of a reductionist anti-racism. Jews themselves cannot be victims of racism, not only because they are now "white", but also because they support a supposedly racist ideology (Zionism) and a racist state (Israel). On the contrary, Jews have themselves, according to this way of thinking, become the enemies of progress, part of the white power structure, locally and globally, to which all anti-racists are rightly opposed. The outcome is a form of antisemitism that denies its own existence.

Since emancipation there has always been, however, another way of thinking on the left about Jews and antisemitism. It is one that sees antisemitism as an evil, as a grave problem not just for Jews but for everyone. Jews are not responsible for antisemitism; antisemites are. Jews are not an obstacle to progress; antisemites are. A left that condones antisemitism, colludes with it, facilitates or tries to exploit it, is (from this perspective) disloyal to its own most fundamental universalist values, to the belief that all human beings have the same rights.

This applies at both the local level, inside all democratic societies, and at the global level, in a world of nation-states. After the Holocaust especially, when the Jewish people were nearly entirely wiped out, there is every reason to understand why Jews remain alert to the threat of antisemitism from any quarter, and why they feel the need for their own state, which is what most of the left originally supported and which some of it still does. That part of the left has never been afraid of Jews, nor has it had any need to be afraid of them. What it has always been rightly afraid of are antisemites. Jews have never posed and do not pose a threat to the left, and a left which is afraid of Jews can, from this perspective, only undermine itself.

How easy it will be to reassert this way of thinking on the left and reverse the tide of recent years is hard to predict. In the UK, the Labour Party has undergone a change of leadership in the aftermath of the worst defeat the party had suffered in over half a century. Although it is not wholly clear how much the problem of antisemitism played in this defeat, there is some evidence that the new leadership is determined to take it seriously, to expel overt antisemites from its ranks and to repair its relationship with the Jewish community. Keir Starmer, as leader of the Labour Party, gave an unequivocal response to the findings of the EHRC investigation, which he called a "day of shame" for the party, promising to implement its recommendations in full. Moreover, he insisted it was essential to root out not just overt antisemites but also all those who complained that the accusations against the Labour Party were exaggerated and politically motivated (complaints that echo the old perception of Jews "behaving badly" by exaggerating their suffering). Indeed, when Jeremy Corbyn characteristically mouthed exactly these arguments in his own shameful response to the report (saying the problem was "dramatically overstated for political reasons" by opponents and the media), he was immediately suspended from the party.

If this is a harbinger of things to come, if there is now indeed the recognition that antisemitism is today a serious problem, not only on the right but also on the left, then there are grounds for hope that the fear of Jews in this case may now subside. Then, too, if what has been happening in the UK leads to a rethink about the different forms anti-semitism can take, perhaps that fear may subside across the left as a whole.

A LICENCE TO HATE

Jill Jacobs

IN AN INTERVIEW with Laura Ingraham on Fox News during the presidential campaign in August 2020, President Donald Trump declared, "people that are in the dark shadows" were controlling his rival Vice-President Joseph Biden, Jr. It's not hard to imagine the identity of these shadowy characters. After all, the final advertisement of Trump's 2016 campaign intoned a warning about "those who control the levers of power in Washington", "global special interests" and "a global power structure", all while flashing pictures of George Soros, Janet Yellen and Lloyd Blankfein, three prominent Jews whom the advertisement cast as puppeteers of Secretary Hillary Clinton.

It is no coincidence that antisemitic incidents, including violent ones, rose during Trump's term in office. The Anti-Defamation League reports that in 2019 the number of incidents hit an all-time high since tracking began in 1979 and that 90 per cent of extremist murders that same year were committed by people on the right. The white nationalists felt newly emboldened by a president who refused to condemn white nationalism, trafficked openly in racism and xenophobia, and regularly mouthed antisemitic dog whistles easily understood by his supporter base.

In refraining, for the most part, from overt antisemitism, while signalling permission for his base to engage in hate speech and even violence, Trump followed the lead of generations of kings and czars who pretended to protect the Jewish community, while deflecting blame for antisemitic attacks on the masses.

Trump's campaign advertisement, and ominous references to "globalists", have their roots in longstanding antisemitic conspiracy theories depicting Jews as a secret global power structure attempting to undermine the world order. Wilhelm Marr, the German politician and writer who coined the term antisemitism, wrote in 1879: "Jews have seized the dictatorship of the state finance system and have inoculated it with the Semitic spirit of manipulation and management... We are the vanquished; we are the subjugated... To Semitism belongs world mastery."

Hatred of Jews had long been based in Christian attempts to explain why Jews persist in following their ancient tradition, rather than accepting Jesus Christ as lord and saviour. Even in places with few actual Jews, Christian thinkers and leaders often conjured up a Jewish other in such a way as to justify Christian supersessionist theology, which claims that a new covenant through Jesus Christ has replaced the covenant with the Jewish people, and that the Jewish Bible should now be read through the lens of the Christian Bible. But atheists and anti-Christian thinkers, Marr among them, needed a different rationale for antipathy toward Jews, especially as these Jews increasingly assimilated and blended in with non-Jewish society during a period of emancipation in the 18th century, when they began to win civil and political rights. This is how racially based antisemitism emerged, asserting that Jews were inherently and racially different from Europeans, not simply adherents of a different religious tradition.

In the Trump era, the conspiracy theory turned newly deadly. In 2017, white nationalists arrived in Charlottesville, Virginia, ostensibly to protect the statue of Confederate General Robert E Lee from a proposal before the city council to remove it. Nostalgia for slavery is solidly grounded in racism, and should – on the face of it – have nothing to do with antisemitism, which was not a factor in the US Civil War. Yet when these armed protestors marched through the city, they chanted "Jews will not replace us", summoning generations of conspiracy theories about Jewish plots against white America.

In October 2018, a white supremacist terrorist murdered 11 worshippers at the Tree of Life synagogue in Pittsburgh. He specifically chose a synagogue celebrating "Refugee Shabbat", in partnership with HIAS, a Jewish agency that has been resettling Jewish and non-Jewish refugees in the US for more than 100 years. Moments before the attack, he posted on social media, "HIAS likes to bring invaders in that kill our people. I can't sit by and watch my people get slaughtered. Screw your optics, I'm going in."

❖ ❖ ❖

White nationalists in the United States have responded to the increased diversity of America, and the rise of political leaders of colour – especially President Barack Obama – with fear about the endangerment of their own form of life. By stirring up panic about a "white genocide", these extremists attempt to frame their own racism in human rights language, by falsely casting "white" as a coherent ethnic or national group, and by suggesting the existence of a nefarious plot, known as the "great replacement", to eliminate white people. This belief is summed up in the white nationalists' "14 words" slogan: "We must secure the existence of our people and a future for white children." Who hatched this evil plot of "white genocide"? As always, the primary suspects are the Jews. White nationalists draw on earlier tropes, such as the portrait in the infamous antisemitic tract *The Protocols of the Elders of Zion*, of the Jews as a secret cabal controlling world affairs, or Russian portrayals of the Jews as somehow simultaneously fomenting the Bolshevik revolution and protecting capitalism, to warn of a secret Jewish plot to flood the United States with non-white immigrants, and to promote the advancement of Black people.

This ideology also echoes the emergence of antisemitism in 19th-century Germany, following the increased integration of Jews into German society. Once Jews began to achieve emancipation, often taking on professions formerly forbidden to Jews, wearing German (or other western) dress, speaking German or other vernaculars and sometimes even converting to Christianity, antisemites feared an alien group surreptitiously infecting German society. As philosopher Karl Eugen Dühring wrote in 1881: "A Jewish question would still exist, even if every Jew were to turn his back on his religion and join one of our major churches... It is precisely the baptized Jews who infiltrate furthest, unhindered in all sectors of society and political life." This fear parallels the contemporary warning by American white nationalists that Jews are trying to pass as white in order to undermine white society. One white supremacist Telegram channel, called "The Noticer", has become infamous for "outing" Jews who reveal themselves as such on social media. Like today's white nationalists, 19th-century antisemites equated Jews with liberal politics and with everything that signalled societal change. As historian David Sorkin writes: "Anti-Semitism became a kind of 'cultural code' signalling the rejection of democracy, civil society, and the Jews' emancipation. Anti-Semitism served many as the bridge to post-liberal politics. It gave coherence and concreteness to reactionary right-wing ideology and proto-fascist politics."

While the Pittsburgh terrorist was correct about the American-Jewish community's overall sympathy towards refugees and immigrants, this position comes from empathy and from historical memory of multiple displacements throughout history, from Jerusalem, Spain, Portugal, England, Germany and elsewhere. Most Jews recognise in President Trump's casting of Latino immigrants as drug dealers, murderers and rapists an echo of the fear of Jewish refugees articulated in the 1940s by a spokesperson for the Blue Star Mothers, who warned of "200,000 Communist Jews at the Mexican border waiting to get into this country. If they are admitted, they will rape every woman and child that is left unprotected".

Conspiracies about Jews plotting to undermine white Christian society by manipulating people of colour are hardly new. In the 1960s, the Ku Klux Klan charged the Jews with orchestrating the civil rights movement. A series of attempted and successful attacks on southern synagogues in the 1950s, most famously the firebombing of The Temple in Atlanta, sought to punish Jews for their advocacy for the rights of Black people. The more polite John Birch Society publicly laid the blame on "communists", at the time a euphemism for Jews in the right-wing imagination. In 1996, the Aryan Nations' "Declaration of Independence" accused the "Zionist Occupied Government" of sins ranging from "wag[ing] war on the people and sovereign states of the south" to "engag[ing] in systemic genocide of the White race... through a rigorous system of forced integration/assimilation" to "excit[ing] alien domestic insurrections".

Like the John Birch Society, President Trump kept his antisemitism subtle, though easily understood by his audience. In the summer before the 2016 presidential election, Trump tweeted a picture of Secretary Hillary Clinton surrounded by money in front of a Jewish star overlaid with the words "Most corrupt candidate ever". Challenged on this antisemitic imagery, Trump responded that he thought that the six-corner figure was a "Sheriff's Star". When former economic advisor Gary Cohn left the White House, Trump commented: "He may be a globalist, but I like him." The term "globalist" has a long history as an antisemitic slur, for example in the warning of the antisemitic forgery *The Protocols of the Elders of Zion* that "the nations of the West are being brought under international control". In response to the 2017 Charlottesville rally, in which a white nationalist drove a car into a crowd of protestors, murdering Heather Heyer, Trump remarked that there were "very fine people on both sides". In 2016, when CNN correspondent Jake Tapper pressed Trump on whether he would reject the endorsement of former KKK Grand Wizard David Duke, then-candidate Trump professed never to have heard of Duke or of white supremacy. Trump employed this same technique of feigning ignorance in October 2020 when NBC News reporter Savannah Guthrie repeatedly pressed him to denounce the antisemitic conspiracy theory QAnon.

Of course, target number one of Trump's antisemitic dog whistles was George Soros. For antisemites, Soros represents the quintessential Jew – a billionaire immigrant who made his money in banking and supports liberal causes. Conspiracy theories popular on the right have accused Soros of paying protestors, of organising and funding a caravan of asylum seekers from Central America, and of placing bricks along protest routes to encourage violence. Former New York City mayor Rudy Giuliani tweeted in the summer of 2020 that Soros's donations to racial justice organisations demonstrate that the philanthropist is "intent on destroying our government for some sick reason of his that goes back to his sick background". Trump often amplified these conspiracies, including tweeting that Soros was paying those who protested the appointment of Supreme Court Justice Brett Kavanaugh, at the same time that white supremacists were distributing antisemitic flyers threatening the Jewish lawyers representing Dr Christine Blasey Ford, who accused Kavanaugh of sexual assault.

Those who defended Trump against charges of antisemitism pointed first to the fact that his daughter, son-in-law and their children are Jewish; and second, to his support for the government of Israeli prime minister Benjamin Netanyahu. We should dispense immediately with the notion that having Jewish children or grandchildren inoculates one from being an antisemite. After all, Trump has two daughters and a wife, yet openly admits to sexual assault, and has credibly been accused of rape by several women.

Trump's supposed support for the state of Israel initially appeared more confusing, in light of his implicit support for white nationalists. Even many Jews considered him to be pro-Israel, following his decision to defy international consensus by moving the US embassy to Jerusalem prior to a peace agreement that settles the status of Jerusalem; his forcing of normalisation agreements between Israel and certain Gulf states; and his sidelining of Palestinians, including through cutting off aid, closing the PLO mission in Washington, DC and the US consulate in East Jerusalem, and presenting a so-called peace plan that allows for annexation of much of the West Bank without insisting on a sovereign Palestinian state.

In fact, Trump's overtures towards Israel represented a concession to his evangelical Christian base, as well as a boost for the wildly unpopular Benjamin Netanyahu, under indictment in his own country and, in 2020, subject for months on end to almost daily protests in multiple Israeli cities calling on him to resign.

American Jews have long expressed both broad support for the long-term security and well-being of the state of Israel, and for a Palestinian state next to it. The majority of American Jews oppose settlement expansion or unilateral annexation of the West Bank, and the majority also opposed moving the US embassy to Jerusalem.

Evangelical Christians, in contrast, have been reliable supporters of right-wing Israel policy, including the expansion of settlements, most visibly through Pastor John Hagee's Christians United for Israel. This so-called support for Israel stems both from a philosemitism that sees Jews as a quaint biblical artifact, often bearing little understanding of the practices and beliefs of modern Jews, and a belief that Jews must all return to the land of Israel in order to bring about the end times prophecy of the Christian Bible.

Even Trump acknowledged that his Israel policies catered to evangelicals, not to Jews. At a rally in Wisconsin in August 2020, he declared: "We moved the capital of Israel to Jerusalem. That's for the evangelicals. You know, it's amazing with that: the evangelicals are more excited about that than Jewish people. Right, it's incredible."

The irony of Trump's prioritising right-wing Israel policy over the safety of American Jews was on full display through the elevation of Christian pastors committed to supersessionist theology and the conversion of Jews (an antisemitic practice with a long and ugly history), who also support policies that bolster the current Israeli government. Robert Jeffress, an evangelical pastor, has declared that "you can't be saved being a Jew" because "the three greatest Jews in the New Testament: Peter, Paul and Jesus Christ... all said Judaism won't do it. It's faith in Jesus Christ". He offered a prayer at the opening of the Jerusalem embassy and also spoke at the 2019 White House Chanukah Party. The latter choice was particularly galling, as Chanukah celebrates the refusal of Jews to abandon our practices and assimilate into the majority religion.

It may be tempting to view Trump's policy concessions to Prime Minister Netanyahu, and Netanyahu's regular praise of the former US president, as proof of Trump's genuine care for Israel, and even Jews. But rather, the alignment between Trump and Netanyahu fitted more clearly into both men's general affinity for autocrats and anti-democratic populists, including Prime Minister Viktor Orbán, President Jair Bolsonaro and President Vladimir

Putin. Netanyahu, as Trump and others conveniently forget, is not a Jewish community leader, but rather the leader of a country, and specifically a leader who is under indictment for multiple corruption scandals, and who has long relied on incitement to promote his agenda and to protect his political future. Netanyahu has even been willing to stoke antisemitism for his political ends, including spreading conspiracy theories about George Soros and playing down Poland's role in the Holocaust to smooth tensions with Prime Minister Mateusz Morawiecki.

That said, Netanyahu and others on the right (both Jewish and Christian) have successfully equated, in the minds of many, support for specific right-wing Israeli policy – particularly occupation and settlement – with support for Jews.

Nowhere is this more clear than in Trump's December 2019 Executive Order on Combating Antisemitism. This executive order, targeted at college campuses, applies to Jews Title VI of the 1964 Civil Rights Act, which bans discrimination based on race, colour and national origin, and goes on to define antisemitism according to the International Holocaust Remembrance Alliance (IHRA) guidelines and examples, which have been widely adopted internationally.

It is clear that Jews remain subject to antisemitism, and are in need of civil rights protection. However, the Department of Justice, during the Obama administration, already clarified that Title VI "provides protections to Jews, Arab Muslims, Sikhs, and/or members of other religious groups". There was therefore no need for a separate executive order applying Title VI to Jews only.

The basic IHRA definition of antisemitism is clear and unobjectionable: "Antisemitism is a certain perception of Jews, which may be expressed as hatred toward Jews. Rhetorical and physical manifestations of antisemitism are directed toward Jewish or non-Jewish individuals and/or their property, toward Jewish community institutions and religious facilities."

The guidelines go on to offer a number of examples, most of which clearly constitute dangerous antisemitism. These include denying the Holocaust; "calling for, aiding, or justifying the killing or harming of Jews in the name of a radical ideology or an extremist view of religion"; and "making mendacious, dehumanizing, demonizing, or stereotypical allegations... such as, especially but not exclusively, the myth about a world Jewish conspiracy".

Two examples, though, have been used to clamp down on free speech on campus. These are "denying the Jewish people their right to self-determination, eg, by claiming that the existence of a State of Israel is a racist endeavor" and "applying double standards by requiring of it a behavior not expected or demanded of any other democratic nation".

I certainly believe that Jews have a right to self-determination, as do Palestinians and all other peoples. But protecting free speech includes protecting the right of others to voicing opposing opinions – even ones that some of us may find hard to hear. While Jews generally view the establishment of the state of Israel as a modern-day miracle that returned Jews to our ancestral homeland, Palestinians view this event as the "nakba" – a catastrophe that resulted in the displacement of more than 700,000 of their people. We can no more expect Palestinians to be Zionists than we might expect Native Americans to celebrate the arrival of the Pilgrims. But no laws force US history professors to refrain from speaking about the bloody origins of our nation. Campuses should be open environments for difficult conversations and protests, sometimes even with harsh language, free from spurious accusations of discrimination. While calling for the expulsion of all Jews from Israel certainly crosses the line into antisemitism, difficult debates about the origin of the nation do not.

Similarly, the language of "double standards" can be used to stifle free speech. Those who complain of a double standard generally mean that student activism disproportionately focuses on Israel rather than on other countries that also violate international human rights. This is true. It's also true that when I was in college in the mid-1990s, campus activism disproportionately revolved around the Free Tibet movement. I'm sure China was displeased, but I never heard that we shouldn't talk about Tibet without also addressing human rights violations in what was then Yugoslavia. As long as critics – even harsh critics – of Israel are holding it to the same human rights laws and conventions as other UN members (often specifically the Fourth Geneva Convention's articles governing the administration of occupied territories), these critiques do not constitute antisemitism.

Criticism of Israel does sometimes cross the line into antisemitism, for example through the application to Israel or "Zionists" of classic antisemitic tropes such as the visual of the octopus controlling the world with its tentacles; the denial of Jewish history in Israel, such as reference to the "alleged" Temple; or repetition of the antisemitic conspiracy theory that modern Jews are not "real" Jews, but rather descendants of Kazakh converts; or demands that Jewish students on campus disavow any connection to Israel before joining progressive coalitions or taking part in student government.

But criticism of Israel as a country, bound by the same international law as other countries, is not inherently antisemitic. While the Boycott, Divestment, Sanctions movement may trigger Jewish trauma born from the Nazi boycott of Jewish businesses, boycotting a country is not the same as boycotting an ethnic or religious group. Indeed, most of the world already boycotts North Korea and Syria. T'ruah, the rabbinic human rights organisation that I lead, for example, belongs to an international anti-trafficking coalition that has called on clothing companies to cease purchasing cotton from the Uighur region of China. And, of course, boycotts of Israel also apply to the 20 per cent of Israeli citizens who are not Jewish, primarily Palestinians.

Rather than make Jews safer, Trump further transformed Jews into an "other", both by strengthening the hand of white supremacists, who base their entire world view on antisemitism, and by equating American Jews with Israel in such a way that may please evangelicals and right-wing allies of Prime Minister Netanyahu, but that ultimately suggests – as too many leaders have through history – that Jews can never be good citizens of the country where we reside.

While Trump may have lost the presidency, Trumpism will not disappear so easily. Trump himself promises to continue to rile up his followers from the sidelines, while violent white nationalists – many still convinced that the election was stolen – organise online, and push their dangerous ideas into the mainstream.

LIVING WITH THE HOLOCAUST

Tom Segev

SHORTLY AFTER THE Second World War, a small group of Holocaust survivors conspired to kill six million Germans in revenge for the extermination of six million Jews. The idea was to poison the potable water sources in major German cities. It was an atrocious fantasy that never materialised, but over the years became a gripping tale. Readers of *Haaretz*, Israel's leading daily newspaper, recently published a stormy exchange of comments on the matter. Some of them argued that had the post-Holocaust "avengers" carried out their plot, future acts of genocide, from Cambodia to Rwanda, would not have been possible and, most significantly, all enemies of the Jews, including today's Iran, would be deterred for ever from harming the state of

Israel. Other readers argued that such a diabolical operation could only have attested to the age-old antisemitic
image of the Jew as "well poisoner". The debate on the
Haaretz website followed a review of a new and rather sym-
pathetic book on the revenge plotters by Dina Porat, the
chief historian of Israel's official Holocaust Remembrance
Center Yad Vashem.

Similar controversies are quite frequent in Israel,
where Holocaust memory continues to constitute a
major element of the collective identity. Zionist ideology,
which led to the creation of Israel, assumed that antisemitism would haunt the Jews for ever, wherever they live
in the world, hence the need for an independent Jewish
state. Theoretically the establishment of Israel could provide asylum to every Jew in need and thus antisemitism
would no longer have to be regarded first and foremost
as a Jewish problem, but rather a social and moral dis-
ease most countries of the world had to deal with, along
with other forms of bigotry. Actually the very terms Jews,
antisemitism, Israel and Zionism still reflect an awkward
and sensitive labyrinth of contradictions and ideological paradoxes. Israel's declaration of independence cites
antisemitism in general and the Holocaust in particular
among the needs for Jewish statehood, while the basic
national dogma decrees: never again. But over the years it
has become increasingly difficult to distinguish between
genuine statements about the Holocaust, reflecting deep-
rooted existential fears, and manipulative statements
about the Holocaust for political ends. Such differentia-

tion is a paramount requirement for anyone who seeks to understand the Israelis.

In the first 20 years of Israel's existence (1948–1968), three major strategic decisions were made under the impact of the Holocaust. Over the first 18 months, almost a million Jewish immigrants were taken in, nearly twice as many as Israel's original population. There was no adequate housing available for so many newcomers, no jobs, no schools and no hospitals. Israel's ability to survive as an independent state obviously depended on a solid Jewish majority, but the general feeling was that in the wake of the Zionist movement's utter helplessness to rescue a substantial number of Jews during the Holocaust, any Jew who wanted or had to settle in Israel should not be turned down.

Sometime in the mid-1950s, Israel began to develop its own nuclear power. The project reflected a combination of Israeli, French and ironically also some German atomic interests. But the dominant logic behind it was that after the Holocaust the Jewish state must not do without any potentially available means of defence. A Berlin-born scientist who headed the project wrote in a private letter: "I cannot forget that the Holocaust arrived as a surprise to the Jews. The Jewish people cannot afford another such illusion."

In June 1967, many Israelis were suddenly swept by panic, expecting the Egyptian army to "exterminate" Israel within days. Threats to that effect, in Hebrew, were continuously broadcast on Radio Cairo; they caused widespread hysteria and greatly contributed to Israel's decision to strike at Egypt. Official Israeli spokespeople encouraged the comparison between Egypt's President Nasser and Hitler, and within the first hours of the Six-Day War it transpired how far from reality the doomsday scenario had been. But hundreds of private letters Israelis sent prior to the war to relatives and friends abroad reflected a distinct Holocaust desperation. Some of the writers resorted to black humour, quoting a sign that was ostensibly displayed near the exit gate at the main airport: "Would the last person to leave the country please turn off the lights." Municipal rabbis in the meantime prepared public parks and football fields to be used as cemeteries, in preparation for tens, perhaps hundreds, of thousands of casualties. All this was quite authentic. Most of the first Israelis were Holocaust survivors or refugees from Arab countries; many had settled there as a result of earlier waves of antisemite persecution or were descendants of such settlers. Many still are.

Holocaust manipulation presents an infinitely more complex story. Many Israeli leaders have manipulated the Holocaust for political purposes and some may have believed that the Arabs were in fact seeking to complete what Hitler had started. At one time or another nearly every Arab ruler has been compared in Israel with Hitler. Shortly before the invasion of Lebanon in 1982, Prime Minister Menachem Begin wrote to President Ronald Reagan that he was sending the Israeli army to Beirut to capture Adolf Hitler in his bunker, meaning Palestinian leader Yasser Arafat. In 2015, Prime Minister Netanyahu contended that the idea to exterminate the Jews was planted in Hitler's mind by another Palestinian leader, Haj Amin al-Husseini. The ludicrous nature of that statement did not prevent the Israeli premier from comparing the nuclear international agreement with Iran to the agreement that let Hitler take Czechoslovakia in 1938. Similar statements once led author Amos Oz to publish a passionate condemnation under the headline "Hitler is Dead, Mr Prime Minister!" He described the frequent reference to the Nazis as a form of collective paranoia, which was fair enough, but not entirely accurate: often Israelis could be better described as paranoid people on the run from real enemies.

Palestinian leader al-Husseini did in fact seek Nazi Germany's support and travelled to Berlin where he was officially received by Hitler. In those days, the Nazis received massive support from people in the Arab world, including young Anwar Sadat, the future Egyptian president. A pro-Nazi government came to power in Iraq in 1941. After the war, several Arab countries offered refuge to Nazi war criminals and Holocaust deniers. In the 1950s, numerous countries and multinational companies gave in to pressure from the oil-producing Arab countries and joined in an economic boycott against Israel that had severe economic results. Israel felt besieged: at that time one in every three Israelis was a Holocaust survivor.

David Ben-Gurion, Israel's first prime minister, regarded the Holocaust first and foremost as a crime against the state of Israel, for the Jews killed by the Nazis were supposed to have become the strongest segment of the future Israeli society. In accordance with Zionist ideology, Ben-Gurion regarded all the world's Jews as a single nation, and believed that all of them belonged in the Jewish state. The creation of a Jewish majority in Palestine, aiming at an independent Jewish state, inevitably involved the replacement of Arabs. The goal was a Jewish state on as much land as possible, with as many Jews as possible and as few Arabs. Less than a Jewish majority, such as in some kind of "bi-national" arrangement, would not have fulfilled the minimal Zionist aim. Indeed, under Ben-Gurion's leadership, hundreds of thousands of Palestinians were uprooted from their homes during the first Arab-Israeli war of 1947–1948 and the vast majority of them were never allowed to return. "The Arabs don't need to live here, just as an American Jew shouldn't live in America," Ben-Gurion stated in 1950. But life was not that simple: Ben-Gurion was also well aware that without the influence and support of Jews in America, the Jewish state would not become a reality and could not survive. At times, Ben-Gurion even asked himself what better served Zionist aims: powerful and influential Jewish communities in America and other countries or Jews in distress who may be compelled to move to Israel. That was an idea first articulated by Theodor Herzl, the founding father of political Zionism: "The antisemites will be our most steadfast friends," he wrote. "The antisemitic countries will be our allies." An agreement reached in 1933 between the Zionist movement and the government of Nazi Germany facilitated the immigration to Palestine of tens of thousands of German

Jews and thus saved their lives. Agreements to evacuate Jews from eastern Europe and the Islamic countries after the Holocaust also tragically confirmed Herzl's thesis.

What then is authentic and what manipulated? In the early 1950s, the Israeli government discussed a plan to grant posthumous Israeli citizenship to all victims of the Holocaust. Ben-Gurion did not rule out this attempt to monopolise the Holocaust, but eventually the idea was dropped. The Yad Vashem Remembrance Center has encouraged the use of the Hebrew term, Shoah, although Israel is the only country in the world where Hebrew is spoken as an everyday language; most Holocaust victims did not know Hebrew, nor do most of the world's Jews today. Holocaust education in Israel puts much emphasis on the unprecedented uniqueness of the Nazi crimes against the Jews. Genocide studies are hardly known in Israel, and comparisons between Nazi antisemitism and other forms of racism are likely to be denounced as a form of Holocaust denial.

Every year, nearly 40,000 Israeli high-school students travel to Auschwitz and some other extermination camps in Poland. Israeli society is deeply divided and the educational system reflects many of the country's political and ideological controversies. Most of the students are expected to recharge their patriotic batteries there. Waving the Israeli flag at the entrance to the gas chambers and singing the national anthem, they will be told by specially trained guides, that "Never again" requires not only military might, but also an obligation to remember that Israel constitutes the only rightful answer to antisemitism and is still in danger of annihilation.

Some of the students are expected to recharge their humanistic batteries in Auschwitz. They too will wave the national flag, but will hear more about the humanistic lessons of the Holocaust, including the need to fight racism and protect human rights. They may hear of non-Jewish groups who were persecuted by the Nazis such as the Roma and homosexuals. Some of them may even be told of the 1956 Kafr Qasim massacre, in which close to 50 Arab-Israeli villagers, among them women and children, were gunned down by a contingent of the armed border police, because they had returned from work half an hour after the start of the daily curfew. The outrage led to a series of criminal trials and convictions; the perpetrators claimed that they had followed orders. Their final verdict bequeathed Israel the so-called "Black Flag" doctrine, which has remained the Holocaust's most significant lesson. Accordingly, a soldier is required to refuse a manifestly illegal order. A German-born judge, Benjamin Halevi, defined such an order graphically: "The hallmark of manifest illegality is that it must wave like a black flag over the given order, a warning that says: forbidden!" In 1967, Israeli soldiers fighting in the Six-Day War said that the doctrine had in fact had a restraining effect on their behaviour towards the Palestinian population.

In those days, Israel was widely recognised as the only democracy in the Middle East, "a villa in the jungle", as Israelis liked to describe their country. In reality, however, following the war of 1948 and for nearly two decades, Arabs living in Israel were subjected to severe restrictions, making them second-class citizens, at least until 1966. Shortly afterwards, Israel occupied the West Bank and Gaza, and the Palestinians were subjected to systematic and often cruel violations of their civil and human rights, at times amounting to brutal atrocities. Over five decades later, they still are.

The long-lasting, passionate and occasionally even violent internal Israeli controversy over the future of the Palestinian territories has often manifested itself in the country's Holocaust discourse. On the one hand, Arab terrorist attacks have been described as acts of Nazi antisemitism, and on the other, Israel's occupation policy has been compared to the German occupation of Europe. On Holocaust Memorial Day in 2016, none other than the Israeli army's deputy chief of staff, Major General Yair Golan, made a speech in which he drew a parallel between Israel and Nazi Germany. The implication was that half a century of oppression in the West Bank and Gaza was inevitably eroding Israeli democracy in a way that was similar to what happened in Germany in the 1930s. In a particularly grotesque display of Holocaust manipulation, Israeli politicians have at times compared each other to Hitler. "Menachem Begin is a classical Hitlerist type," David Ben-Gurion once wrote about the leader of the right-wing opposition and future prime minister.

In 1975, the UN General Assembly adopted a resolution that defined Zionism as a form of racism and racist discrimination. Israel described the resolution as a flagrant display of antisemitism and put its revocation at the top of its diplomatic priorities. In the 1990s, a wave of Holocaust denial swept the world, followed by an increase in antisemitism incidents, including several murderous attacks on Jewish schools and synagogues. Although mostly unrelated to the situation in Israel, this upsurge of antisemitism led in 1991 to the revocation of the UN anti-Zionist resolution. In 1998, an intergovernmental taskforce for Holocaust research and education was founded, later called the International Holocaust Remembrance Alliance (IHRA). All members of the organisation were committed to the struggle against both antisemitism and Holocaust denial, but no immediate agreement could be reached on the definition of either. There followed a multitude of open-and-closed door consultations and negotiations, generating drafts and counter-drafts that evolved into one of the most engrossing and often heated intellectual, moral and political debates in modern times. One of the major disagreements stemmed from Israel's efforts to include anti-Zionism in the definition of antisemitism.

Under Netanyahu, Israel shifted to the right at the same time as a number of other countries. Conditions in Gaza under Hamas deteriorated atrociously; the number of Israeli settlers in the West Bank reached nearly half a million. The so-called "two-state solution" to the Israeli–Palestinian conflict became obsolete. As a result, criticism of Israel grew, particularly in the United States and Europe. In 2005, an international movement was created that campaigned for various forms of boycott against Israel. Boycott, Divestment, Sanctions (BDS) is an amalgamation of groups with varying agendas, sizes and means of operation. By that time, however, Israel had become a dramatic success story, and under Netanyahu the country was better off than ever before, economically, militarily and diplomatically. Thus, unlike the anti-Israel boycott in the 1950s, organisations such as BDS have been incapable of causing real harm to the country. Still, Netanyahu greatly inflated the organisation's potential danger and ordered a grandiose counter-offensive. Claiming that BDS represents a new form of antisemitism, aimed at the destruction of Israel, one of Netanyahu's cabinet ministers was put in charge of a new body called the Ministry of Strategic Affairs. A series of legal, diplomatic and other measures were taken, some of them clandestine.

These efforts were only partially successful. In 2016, the IHRA included several forms of Israel-bashing in its working definition of antisemitism, among them: "Denying the Jewish people their right to self-determination, eg by claiming that the existence of a State of Israel is a racist endeavor" and "Drawing comparisons of contemporary Israeli policy to that of the Nazis". Israel would have liked stronger formulations.

Most Jews of the world share a sense of solidarity with Israel and sympathy for it; indeed, at times the oppression of the Palestinians has been criticised with genuine concern for Israel's future as a Jewish and democratic country. Israel depends to a considerable extent on its international image, and criticism from abroad can sometimes curb its harsh treatment of the Palestinians. However, not all Jews are Zionists. A majority of Jews have never been inclined to live in Palestine or emigrated to America and other countries. Moreover, some of the most ardent critics of Zionist ideology belong to Orthodox Jewish communities in America and even in Israel. Hence a negative attitude towards Israel or Zionist ideology should not be branded automatically as a display of antisemitism. On the other hand, some of Israel's strongest support in America comes from the so-called evangelical Bible belt and involves the obviously antisemitic aspiration that all Jews will ultimately abandon their faith and see the light of Jesus Christ.

Some racists have in fact chosen to disguise their antisemitism as criticism of Israel and Zionism. Antisemitic agitation has often been directed against the Jews of Israel, particularly by radical Islamist terror organisations. But some of Israel's policies and actions, particularly in the Palestinian territories occupied in 1967, have also triggered antisemitism, agitation and terror against Jews in other countries, including Austria, Argentina, Belgium and India. The issue continues to be in dispute; not even the editors of Wikipedia have been able to resolve it. According to Wikipedia's English text "some sources" view anti-Zionism as a cover for modern-day antisemitism, but critics have challenged that position "as a tactic to silence criticism of Israeli policies". Three Jewish-American intellectuals are quoted to the effect that there is no correlation between the two terms. In the German Wikipedia version, the entry first identifies "frequent correlations between anti-Zionism and antisemitism" and states: "Anti-Zionism can hardly be distinguished from antisemitism".

Human rights violations in many countries are frequently scrutinised and criticised by international organisations, NGOs and the media. Many allegations are anchored in solid foundations, as they often are in the case of Israel. The situation in the Holy Land has always been particularly close to the hearts of the international community, and Israel is relatively easy to monitor. Moreover, Israel has always claimed to share the humanistic value system of the west, including international law, and over the years has acquired the respect of most of the democratic world. Thus when violating legal and moral obligations, it has often been judged more severely than countries that have not claimed allegiance to western liberalism. Israel-bashing, coming from such totalitarian countries as Turkey or North Korea, attests to the hypocrisy and double standards that often sneak into human rights discourse.

There are few countries in the world that don't have dark and shameful chapters in their past, but they should be judged today mainly by the lessons for the future they have drawn from their history. Some countries have conducted critical self-examination of their past and even formally apologised for historic injustices. In this respect, Germany offers one of the most admirable examples. Israel has always denied any responsibility for either the past or the present Palestinian tragedy. At this time a just solution to the Israeli–Palestinian conflict seems as far off as ever, but recognising the injustices of the past seems an essential step on the road to some better future. However, at the time of writing, both genuine and manipulated attitudes to the Holocaust and antisemitism preclude such a soul-searching process.

AFTERWORD

An Interview with David Nirenberg

Jo Glanville

SHORTLY AFTER 9/11, the historian David Nirenberg was riding the subway from Penn Station to New York University – on a line that now ended under the rubble of the World Trade Center. There were two other occupants in an otherwise empty carriage, and they were discussing the cause of the terrorist attack. "Both of them agreed that the reason was the Jews," he recalls. "They gave different arguments. One of them said it was because the Jews had turned New York into a symbol of greed and that was why everyone hated New York. The other's argument was that they had killed Christ: that was why everyone hated them, and targeted New York because of its Jews." Nirenberg was struck that a similar conversation could have taken place in medieval Barcelona between citizens discussing the causes of the plague. Though centuries apart, in both cases people were trying to understand a new fear. "Obviously they're not the same – this isn't an argument about eternal antisemitism, it's a question of how certain forms of making sense of the world continue to adapt so they can continue to make sense of the world. You can only take that seriously if you grant that these ideas do help these individuals make sense of the new challenges they're facing, of the new world they're in. And that these ideas do owe something to the past."

The encounter was the seed for a book, *Anti-Judaism*, which was published in 2013. Only one publisher, Norton, showed interest in Nirenberg's book proposal. At the time, antisemitism was not on the agenda. Not long after the book's publication, however, antisemitic incidents began to rise. "It took me a long time to write the book, partly because I was embarrassed to write it in the sense that none of my peers were thinking this is a key problem that a person should be thinking about," he says. "A book that I started in 2001, about a problem no one really thought about much then, has become a book about a problem that is very much with us. I think we should always be surprised when our anxieties or prophecies correspond in any way to the future."

Nirenberg's book is essential reading: an original and enlightening explanation of why the hatred of Jews persists. He traces its roots to the ancient world, through Christianity, Islam and into the emergence of western political philosophy. He demonstrates that from the earliest days of Christianity, Judaism was used as a framework for thinking about the world. The Jews embodied the negative of everything that Christianity aspired to – they represented worldly materialism and carnality while Christianity represented the spirit and freedom. This formulation became a critical way in which Christianity defined itself. Charges of "judaizing" were, for example, used as a slur by Christians to delegitimize other Christians: critically, it did not mean that opponents were Jewish, but that they were deploying an argument that was unacceptable to their "true" Christian rivals.

This way of thinking about Jews and Judaism – as a conceptual framework – was adopted by early Enlightenment thinkers, adapting a theological argument into secular terms. Nirenberg charts its journey through Voltaire, Kant, Hegel and Marx into social science, economics and even mathematics. Anti-Judaism became embedded in western thought – it was a tool of critique with such a long history that everyone understood what it symbolised and continued to reaffirm those symbols. In a lawsuit before the English civil war, a judge criticised the king's opponents for holding "a kind of judaizing opinion"; Spinoza (himself Jewish) saw Judaism as the enemy of reason (similar to Christianity's view of Jews as the enemies of revelation, notes Nirenberg); for Kant, Judaism represented an incorrect attitude toward the material world (once again echoing Christian thinking) far from the path towards truth. "Judaism is ... not only a religion but a category," writes Nirenberg. "A set of ideas and attributes with which non-Jews can make sense of and criticize their world."

When I interviewed David Nirenberg in October 2021, the best-selling Irish novelist Sally Rooney had just announced that her latest novel would not be translated into Hebrew. She said that she did not want to "accept a new contract with an Israeli company that does not publicly distance itself from apartheid and support the UN-stipulated rights of the Palestinian people". Her first two novels had been published in Hebrew. She clarified that she did not object to her book being translated into the Hebrew language, so long as it was compliant with the Boycott, Divestment, Sanctions movement's institutional boycott guidelines. It's unlikely, however, that anyone other than an Israeli publisher would have access to a Hebrew-reading public. Sally Rooney is of course entitled to support any cause she wishes to adopt. Yet the act of preventing her book from being published in one language only singles out Hebrew as a language of particular harm, even if that was not Rooney's intention. It is an action that has a powerful resonance, continuing the role of Jews through history that Nirenberg reveals in his book: Jews, in this case Israel, represent a singular instance of wrongdoing, beyond Iran, Saudi Arabia, Egypt or any other state guilty of egregious human rights abuse in the neighbourhood.

"Why does Sally Rooney, who lives in a very complicated world, understand the largest threat confronting the world in terms of Israel and understand it convincingly enough that she thinks she's doing good in the world by singling out Israel?" responded Nirenberg, when I asked him for his opinion. "I think that's not a very dissimilar question – I'm going to be provocative here – to why so many Europeans in the 1930s came to believe, to accept, to be convinced that the Jews were the greatest danger to their own well being, to the good, in fact so convinced that they were willing to be complicit in the elimination of that danger.

"The question has to be how do the Jews, or Israel, become a convincing explanation of what is wrong with the world? And that's a big challenge because we always get stuck on reality. For Hannah Arendt it was economic – the Jews are hated because they're so rich. Today the most frequently invoked reality is Israel – the Jews are hated because Israel is a colonial, occupying, apartheid state. But the real is not the actual driver of this logic. It's not the set of conditions that make this logic so convincing. That set of conditions is already shaped by how we've learnt to think."

Nirenberg points to replacement theory (the conspiracy theory that there is a plot to eliminate the white population in the US or Europe and replace it with non-white immigrants) as one of the current examples of contemporary anti-Judaism. "Jews will not replace us," was one of the chants at the Charlottesville demonstration in 2017 when Heather Heyer was killed. In 2018, the billionaire philanthropist George Soros was accused of supporting a caravan of migrants to enter the US from Central America, a conspiracy theory that inflamed the far right with lethal consequences.

"It is one up-to-date way of trying to explain what feels like challenges to western culture," Nirenberg continues.

"Migration, civil rights, the mobility of peoples are increasingly seen by all sides of the debate as a Jewish problem. So, for example, Muslim immigrants to Paris, even second or third generation, often think of their challenges as having something to do with Israel and they act out against Judaism in Paris or France as a symbol of what oppresses them. But similarly French nativists also understand their problems as having to do with Israel, meaning the Jews. It's how we're thinking about injustice and inequality and decolonisation, and intersectionality. Those are really important ideals, and we find ourselves very often thinking about them in terms of Jews, Judaism and Israel. That's a curious thing. And it's even more curious when you realise how old that tendency is — that is the tendency of imagining the intersection between lots of identities in the world and Judaism.

"These are very old ideas, yet we encounter them as new in every generation and we feel like we've discovered them, and since we don't pay attention to their history, we are not inoculated against their dangers. It's a little bit like immune systems. I think if we were more aware, more willing to be open to the ways in which we have succumbed to these projections in the past, made these mistakes before, we could perhaps better resist their attraction. There's a very interesting question why it's so hard to resist that attraction."

Nirenberg's deeply researched portrait of how western thought was captured and even shaped by the ideal of overcoming Judaism is deeply chilling. It also shows what a fundamental purpose the idea of Jews has served in the development of western culture. It is hardly surprising, with this interpretation, that antisemitism never disappears. It is not only part of the fabric, it has served as an explanation of the world we live in and, perhaps most disturbingly in the face of rising antisemitism, even as a tool for imagining a better world – from Marx's belief that liberation means emancipation from Judaism to Goebbels' desire to rid the world of "rampant Jewish intellectualism". The terrors of Nazi Germany were, writes Nirenberg in *Anti-Judaism*, the product of "a history that had encoded the threat of Judaism into some of the basic concepts of human thought".

"Today, or any moment where the political becomes both an explicit object of anxiety and critique, either because it's felt to be too powerful or it's felt to be trembling on its foundations, these concepts about Judaism become really useful again," says Nirenberg. "And that's another way of thinking about the situation we find ourselves in today, at a moment in which our political forms are very much themselves the object of critique. Is liberalism an adequate form? Is democracy an adequate form? Is the surveillance state the epitome of human subjection to law? In such moments western societies have often turned to thinking about Judaism, and anti-Judaism becomes a powerful discourse."

Whether, as Nirenberg suggests, we can resist the attraction to a deeply embedded way of thinking through understanding its history is another question. For the moment, his thesis can at least help us appreciate the scale of the challenge.

BIOGRAPHIES

Jo Glanville (editor) is a journalist and award-winning editor. Her writing on culture and social affairs has been published in the *Guardian, London Review of Books, New York Times, Observer, Times Literary Supplement, Financial Times* and *Prospect*, among other publications. A former BBC current affairs producer, she has made a number of documentaries on the Holocaust and on the Middle East. She was editor of Index on Censorship and is a former director of the charity English PEN.

Olga Grjasnowa was born in Baku, Azerbaijan, in 1984. She graduated from the German Institute for Literature in Leipzig and has received funding from the Rosa Luxemburg Foundation, as well as travel grants from the Robert Bosch Foundation in 2011 and 2019. Her 2012 debut novel *Der Russe ist einer, der Birken liebt* (*All Russians Love Birch Trees*, tr. Eva Bacon) was awarded the Klaus Michael Kühne Prize, the Hermann Lenz Grant and the Anna Seghers Prize. Her novels *Die juristische Unschärfe einer Ehe* and *Gott ist nicht* *schüchtern* followed in 2014 and 2017. She received the Berlin Senate's work stipend for literature in 2014 and 2019. All her books have been dramatised for the stage, and translated into a total of 15 languages. Her novel *Der verlorene Sohn* was published in 2020, when her own dramatisation premiered at the Berliner Ensemble theatre.

Mikołaj Grynberg is a photographer and writer with a background in psychology. His photographs have been exhibited worldwide. He is the author of the photography books *Many Women* (2009) and *Auschwitz What Am I Doing here?* (2010), the documentary books *Survivors of the 20th Century* (2012), *I Accuse Auschwitz: Family Stories* (2014) and *The Book of Exodus* (2018), and the short story collection *Rejwach* (2017). He has worked for many years on the historical and social issues of Polish Jews in the 20th century. He addresses all of his work through the particular perspective of dialogue, concentrating on personal connection and openness to the experiences and stories of others. He was nominated for the Julian Tuwim Literary Prize (2019) for his complete body of work.

Jill Jacobs is the executive director of T'ruah, which mobilises more than 2,000 rabbis and cantors to protect and advance human rights in North America, Israel and the occupied Palestinian territories. She is the author of *Where Justice Dwells: A Hands-On Guide to Doing Social Justice in Your Jewish Community* and *There Shall Be No Needy: Pursuing Social Justice through Jewish Law and Tradition*, both published by

Jewish Lights. She holds rabbinic ordination and an MA in Talmud from the Jewish Theological Seminary, where she was a Wexner Fellow an MS in Urban Affairs from Hunter College and a BA from Columbia University. She is also a graduate of the Mandel Institute Jerusalem Fellows Program. She lives in New York with her husband, Rabbi Guy Austrian, and their two daughters.

Natasha Lehrer has degrees from Oxford University and the University of Paris VIII. She won a Rockower journalism award in 2016, and the Scott Moncrieff Translation Prize in 2017 for her co-translation of *Suite for Barbara Loden* by Nathalie Léger. Several of her book translations have been shortlisted for major prizes. Her criticism and essays have appeared in the *Times Literary Supplement*, *Guardian*, *Nation*, *Observer* and *Haaretz*, among other publications. She is a contributing editor at *Jewish Quarterly*.

Tom Segev is a leading historian and one of Israel's most distinguished journalists. He was born in Jerusalem in 1945 to parents who fled Nazi Germany. Segev holds a BA in History and Political Science from the Hebrew University and a PhD in History from Boston University. In 2000 and 2010, Segev's books were included in the *New York Times'* Best Books of the Year lists. In 2001, Segev's *One Palestine, Complete* (2000) was the first title ever to win the National Jewish Book Award in two categories. Formerly a reporter and columnist for *Haaretz*, Segev has published nine works, most recently *A State At All Costs: The Story of David Ben-Gurion* (2018).

Philip Spencer is Emeritus Professor in Holocaust and Genocide Studies at Kingston University, where he taught for many years. He is a Visiting Professor in Politics at Birkbeck College, where he is also a Research Associate of the Pears Institute for the Study of Antisemitism. He is the author of a number of works, including *Nationalism – A Critical Introduction* (2002) and *Nations and Nationalism* (2005) (both with Howard Wollman), *Genocide since 1945* (2012) and *Antisemitism and the Left – on the Return of the Jewish Question* (2017) (with Robert Fine). He is currently writing a longer history of genocide.

Daniel Trilling is a London-based journalist and the author of *Lights in the Distance: Exile and Refuge at the Borders of Europe* (2018) and *Bloody Nasty People: the Rise of Britain's Far Right* (2012).

Sean Gasper Bye (translator) has translated books from Polish by Lidia Ostałowska, Filip Springer, Małgorzata Szejnert and Szczepan Twardoch. A native of Bucks County, Pennsylvania, he studied Modern Languages at University College London and International Studies at the School of Oriental and African Studies. He spent five years as Literature and Humanities Curator at the Polish Cultural Institute New York. He is a winner of the Asymptote Close Approximations Prize and a recipient of a National Endowment for the Arts translation fellowship.

Katy Derbyshire (translator) comes from London and moved to Berlin as an adult. She translates contemporary German writers including Olga Grjasnowa, Sandra Hoffmann, Heike Geissler and Angela Steidele. Her translation of Clemens Meyer's *Bricks and Mortar* was nominated for the MAN Booker International Prize and won her the Straelen Translation Prize in 2018. Katy co-hosts the bimonthly Dead Ladies Show in Berlin and is now publisher at the V&Q Books imprint, exporting remarkable writing from Germany to the UK and Ireland.

ACKNOWLEDGEMENTS

I'D LIKE TO THANK all the writers and translators who contributed to this anthology – I've learnt a lot from all of them. Emma Craigie generously invited me to talk about antisemitism at The Chapel in 2018, which resulted in this book. I'm grateful to Aurea Carpenter and Rebecca Nicolson at Short Books for giving me the chance to edit the anthology, to William Pimlott for his great attention to detail in the final stages and to Evie Dunne. It's also been a great pleasure working with Jill Bialosky and Drew Elizabeth Weitman at W. W. Norton for the American edition of the anthology. Very particular thanks to Sascha Feuchert at the Arbeitsstelle Holocaustliteratur, University of Giessen, whose friendship and advice throughout have been invaluable. I've also appreciated the guidance and suggestions of David Feldman and Anthony Bale at the Pears Institute for the Study of Antisemitism, Birkbeck College, University of London, when this book was in an earlier incarnation. And I'm indebted to the support of Malu Halasa, Daniel Lubin, Tamara Joffe, Antonia Lloyd Jones, Wenzel Michalski, Rosie Goldsmith, Juliet Mabey, Mike Harris, Nick Cohen, Natasha Lehrer, Peter Beinart, Renate Samson, Ziyad Marar, Felix Luckau, Tim de Lisle, and Mark, Liz and Toby Glanville. My father, Brian Glanville, remains my first and last discussion partner on antisemitism, never wearying of the subject and always my touchstone.

Jo Glanville

ENDNOTES

INTRODUCTION

Page VII

"from President Trump's rumour-mongering... to Labour Party members in the UK accusing Jews of various Zionist plots": Cody Fenwick, "Trump has a long history of anti-Semitic dog whistles", salon.com, 30 October 2018; Steerpike, "Labour's pockets of anti-Semitism: the evidence", *Spectator,* 30 March 2018

"In Europe and America, antisemitic incidents have reached an historic high": Community Security Trust, Antisemitic Incidents Report 2020, Anti-Defamation League, US Antisemitic Incidents Remained at Historic High in 2020, 27 April 2021

Page IX

"Respected actor Maxine Peake": Alexandra Pollard, "Maxine Peake: 'People who couldn't vote Labour because of Corbyn? They voted Tory as far as I'm concerned'", *Independent*, 25 June 2020

"Deborah Lipstadt": Deborah Lipstadt, *Denying the Holocaust*, 1994, New York: Plume, p23; pp56-58

Page X

"As the historian Tony Kushner has shown": Tony Kushner, *The Holocaust and the Liberal Imagination*, Oxford: Wiley,1994, pp133, 227

"Some commentators have put this visibility down to the rise of populist politics": Jonathan Freedland, "The roots of Labour's antisemitism lie deep within the populist left", *Guardian*, 12 July 2019; Peter Pulzer, *The Rise of Political Anti-Semitism in Germany and Austria*, Cambridge MA: Harvard University Press, 1988, p287

"Nor can antisemitism be separated from a rising xenophobia": Narzanin Massoumi, "Why Is Europe So Islamophobic?", *New York Times*, 6 March 2020

Page XI

"Anti-migrant rhetoric influenced Robert Bowers' assault": Adam Serwer, "Trump's Caravan Hysteria Led to This", *Atlantic*, 28 October 2018; Jeremy W Peters, "How Trump-Fed Conspiracy Theories About Migrant Caravan Intersect With Deadly Hatred", *New York Times*, 29 October 2018

"Bowers accused Jews": Lois Beckett, "Pittsburgh shooting: suspect railed against Jews and Muslims on site used by 'alt-right'", *Guardian*, 27 October 2018

"EU survey in 2018": Experiences and perceptions of antisemitism, Second survey on discrimination and hate crime against Jews in the EU, European Union Agency for Fundamental Rights, 2018, pp54-56,

Page XII

"European and American Jews... are perceived as privileged and as white": "Labour and Antisemitism: a Crisis Misunderstood", Ben Gidley, Brendan McGeever, David Feldman, *Political Quarterly*, 10 May 2020; David Hirsh, *Contemporary Left Antisemitism*, Oxford and New York: Routledge, 2018, pp145-146

"Equality and Human Rights Commission's damning report on antisemitism": Equality and Human Rights Commission, Investigation into Antisemitism in the Labour Party, October 2020

"The scale of the problem was 'dramatically overstated', Corbyn claimed": Peter Walker and Jessica Elgot, "Jeremy Corbyn rejects overall findings of EHRC report on antisemitism in Labour", *Guardian*, 29 October 2020

"Jews were apparently exaggerating their victimhood or even (once again) behind a conspiracy": Kerry-Anne Mendoza, editor of The Canary, claimed on BBC Radio 4's *PM*, programme, 29 October 2020, that a "tiny group of obscenely powerful people" were behind the accusations of antisemitism, "a group of people who have taken the dark decision to weaponise Jewish trauma in order to conduct a factional, political battle".

"A statutory public body identified a culture": EHRC report, p100

Page XIII

"The International Holocaust Remembrace Alliance (IHRA) definition": "Antisemitism is a certain perception of Jews, which may be expressed as hatred toward Jews. Rhetorical and physical manifestations of antisemitism are directed toward Jewish or non-Jewish individuals and/or their property, toward Jewish community institutions and religious facilities." Working Definition of Antisemitism, International Holocaust Remembrance Alliance, holocaustremembrance.com, 2018

"A number of leading commentators and lawyers": Counsel's opinion on the IHRA definition, Hugh Tomlinson QC, freespeechonisrael.org, 8 March 2017; Geoffrey Robertson QC, Opinion "Anti-Semitism: the IHRA definition and its consequences for freedom of expression", prc.org.uk, 31 August 2018; David Feldman, "The government should not impose a faulty definition of antisemitism on universities", *Guardian*, 2 December 2020

Page XIV

"Stephen Sedley": Stephen Sedley, "Defining Anti-Semitism", *London Review of Books*, 4 May 2017

"Gavin Williamson": Nicola Woolcock, "Gavin Williamson threatens funding cuts over universities' antisemitism failures", *The Times*, 9 October 2020

"A lead drafter of the definition": Kenneth Stern, "I drafted the definition of antisemitism. Rightwing Jews are weaponizing it", *Guardian*, 13 December 2019

Page XV

"Popularised in the late 19th century by Wilhelm Marr": Moshe Zimmerman, *Wilhelm Marr, The Patriarch of Anti-Semitism*, New York and Oxford: Oxford University Press, 1986, p89; Peter Pulzer, 1988, p47

"Peter Beinart": Peter Beinart, "Yavne: A Jewish Case for Equality in Israel-Palestine", jewishcurrents.org, 7 July 2020

FRANCE'S MODEL MINORITY

Page 22

"As James McAuley noted": James McAuley, "The brutal killing of a Holocaust survivor raises anti-Semitism fears in France", *Washington Post*, 26 March 2018

Page 24

"As historian Maurice Samuels makes clear": Maurice Samuels, *The Right to Difference: French Universalism and the Jews*, Chicago: University of Chicago Press, 2016, p5

Page 25

"The problem of acknowledging the specificity of racism without acknowledging the specificity of race": Natasha Lehrer, "The Unique Problem of

Antisemitism That Won't Go Away", *Plus 61J* magazine, 12 April 2018

Pages 25-26

"French National Institute of Statistics and Economic Studies, was at pains to point out recently": Sylvie Le Minez, "Oui, la statistique publique produit des statistiques ethniques", *Insee*, 31 July 2020

Page 27

"As a figure in the rhetoric of the 1789 revolution": Sarah Hammerschlag, *The Figural Jew: Politics and Identity in Postwar French Thought*, Chicago: Chicago University Press, 2010, p7

"The Jew was 'a tribal remnant'": ibid., p7

Page 28

"As Maurice Samuels reminds us, Jews were able": Samuels, p4

"In the words of prominent Jewish philosopher Bernard-Henri Lévy": James McAuley, "France's most famous intellectual urges Jews not to leave", *Washington Post*, 29 February 2016

Page 29

"Daniella Doron, who stresses the nuanced complexity of French-Jewish identity": Daniella Doron, "The Jews of Modern France, a historiographical essay", in Zvi Jonathan Kaplan and Nadia Malinovich (eds), *The Jews of Modern France: Images and Identities*, Brill's Series in Jewish Studies, Volume 56: Leiden and Boston: Brill, 2016, p12

"Sephardi populations began to use communal organisations": Natasha Lehrer, "The Threat to France's Jews", *Guardian*, 15 January 2015

Page 30

"Both the LICRA and MRAP": Emmanuel Debono, *Aux origines de l'antiracisme. La Ligue internationale contre l'antisémitisme (LICA), 1927-1940, (The Origins of Anti-Racism. The International League*

Against Anti-Semitism (LICA), 1927-1940), foreword by Serge Berstein, Paris, CNRS Editions, 2012

Page 31

"France's main Jewish organisations' response": Shirli Sitbon, "The Dilemma of French Jews and the Fight Against Racism", *Haaretz*, 24 July 2020

"Francis Kalifat, head of the CRIF": ibid.

Page 32

"This has led to 'an extensive reinterpretation of one of republicanism's core values, laïcité'": Emile Chabal, *A Divided Republic: Nation, State and Citizenship in Contemporary France*, Cambridge: Cambridge University Press, 2015, p26

"This brief explanation does not do justice to the protean nature of laïcité": the 1905 law on the Separation of the Churches and the State, which brought laïcité (literally, secularism) into the constitution, is based on three principles: the neutrality of the state, the freedom of religious exercise, and public powers related to the church. Nowadays, however, it is often taken, both popularly and legislatively, to signify state opposition to the manifestation of any signs of religious affiliation.

Page 33

"Finkielkraut's rhetoric": see for example Finkielkraut's notorious interview in *Haaretz*: "What sort of French men are they?", Dror Mishani, Aurelia Smotriez, 16 November 2005

Page 35

"In 1998, historian Paula Hyman presciently observed": Paula E Hyman, *The Jews of Modern France*, Berkeley and Los Angeles: University of California Press, 1998

LOOKING FOR AN ENEMY

Page 38

"Research by the Anti-Defamation League, an American-Jewish campaign group": Anti-Defamation League, "Anti-Semitic Targeting of Journalists During the 2016 Presidential Campaign", 19 October 2016

"Even some prominent Conservative MPs": Rob Merrick, "Theresa May speech 'could have been taken out of Mein Kampf', Vince Cable says", *Independent*, 5 July 2017; Peter Walker, "Tory MP criticised for using antisemitic term 'cultural Marxism'", Guardian, 26 March 2019; Daniel Trilling, "A reckless Tory party is resorting to pantomime authoritarianism", *Guardian*, 11 October 2019

Page 40

"Jewry is a world pest wherever it is found," Tyndall told an interviewer: George Thayer, *The British Political Fringe*, London, Anthony Blond, 1965

Page 42

"The counter-extremism researcher Julia Ebner": Julia Ebner, *Going Dark: The Secret Social Lives of Extremists*, London: Bloomsbury, 2020

"The US author Chip Berlet provides a useful anatomy of the far right's world view": Chip Berlet and Matthew M Lyons, *Right-Wing Populism in America*, New York: Guilford Publications, 2000. I am grateful to the US anti-fascist researcher Spencer Sunshine for pointing me towards this. His own thoughts on the subject can be found at https://www.patreon.com/posts/36706153

Page 46

"The linguist Ruth Wodak argues": Ruth Wodak, "The Radical Right and Antisemitism", in Jens Rydgren (ed.), *The Oxford Handbook of the Radical Right*, Oxford: Oxford University Press, 2018

Page 48

"The late historian Moishe Postone argued that": Moishe Postone, "Anti-Semitism and National Socialism: Notes on the German Reaction to 'Holocaust'", published in *New German Critique* 19: Special Issue 1, Durham, NC: Duke University Press, 1980, pp97-115; available online at https://libcom.org/library/anti-semitism-national-socialism-moishe-postone

THE ASHES ARE STILL WARM

Page 53

"What could not be completed in the gas chambers": Ronen Steinke, *Terror gegen Juden*, Berlin: Berlin Verlag, 2020, p110

"The myth of the lone-wolf perpetrator prevailed": Patrick Guyton, "Die Mär vom frustrierten Einzeltäter", *Heidenheimer Zeitung*, 25 September 2020

Page 55

"Philipp Amthor, an MP for the Christian Democratic Party (CDU) said exactly that in an interview": "Kritik an Antisemitismus in 'muslimischen Kreisen'", n-tv, 27 January 2020

"The numbers are clear, at least on the basis of hate crimes statistics for 2019": https://www.bmi.bund.de/SharedDocs/downloads/DE/veroeffentlichungen/2020/pmk-2019-hasskriminalitaet.pdf;jsessionid=8981E2805BB1EC65A075EBFBEFCFC89C.1_cid364?__blob=publicationFile&v=4

"Police attributed 80 per cent of that year's 1,596 antisemitic crimes to the right-wing spectrum": https://www.bundesregierung.de/resource/blob/975954/774624/035cbc7b70c1e8a1ffdc0d937b829241/71-2-bmi-data.pdf?download=1

Page 56

"Christians have been discriminating against Jews for 2,000 years": Ijoma Mangold, "Rassismus trifft alle Minderheiten", *Die Zeit*, 3 December 2015

Page 57

"Almost half (48 per cent) were of the opinion": "A quarter of Germans have antisemitic thoughts, new survey finds", *The Local*, 24 October 2019

"The statement of the former head of the AFD": "Gauland: NS-Zeit nur ein 'Vogelschiss in der Geschichte'", *Die Zeit*, 2 June 2018

Page 58

"The FAZ newspaper refused to print an advance extract": "Walser erwägt Klage gegen die 'FAZ'", *Der Spiegel*, 29 May 2002

Page 60

"Her appearance was cancelled due to alleged threats from the left": "Veranstalter dementiert Berichte zu Gewaltdrohungen gegen Lisa Eckhart", *Der Standard*, 8 August 2020

Page 61

"The Federal Association of Departments for Research and Information on Antisemitism (RIAS) criticised the routine": Philipp Peyman Engel, "Judenhass unter dem Deckmantel der Satire", *Jüdische Allgemeine*, 4 May 2020

"The journalist Sebastian Hammelehle wrote in Der Spiegel": Sebastian Hammelehle, "Das sind die beiden Autoren, die nicht mit Lisa Eckhart auftreten wollten", *Der Spiegel*, 8 September 2020

Page 62

"Wieso sind in Sachen Humor...voraus?": Lisa Eckhart, "Huch, ich hab' schon wieder einen antisemitischen witz gemacht", BR Kultur-

Bühne, 11 November 2021, https://www.br.de/kultur/gesellschaft/lisa-eckhart-macht-antisemitischen-witz-in-aktuellem-programm-100.html

Page 63

"Police officers calling up the data of people they disagree with...stockpiling weapons": "Abruf von Daten aus Polizeicomputer nun Fall für Datenschutz", *Die Welt*, 7 September 2020; "Illegale Datenabfragen auch von Polizeicomputern in Hamburg und Berlin", *Die Zeit*, 27 August 2020; "Nazi-Devotionalien und Kriegswaffen beschlagnahmt", *Frankfurter Allgemeine*, 23 March 2020; "Hakenkreuze und Tierpornos", *Taz*, 14 October 2020; Anja Laud, "Polizist mit Nazi-Zimmer aufgeflogen", *Frankfurter Rundschau*, 17 January 2019; Muriel Kalisch, Daniel Müller und Holger Stark, "Polizei findet 1,2 Kilo TNT bei mutmaßlichem Rechtsterroristen", *Die Zeit*, 9 October 2020

"Interior Minister Horst Seehofer refusing to allow": Ben Knight, "German minister adamant over police racism study", *Deutsche Welle*, 20 September 2020; "Bericht: Bei der Berliner Polizei gab es eine rassistische Chatgruppe", *Rundfunk Berlin-Brandenburg*, 1 October 2020; "Rechtsextreme WhatsApp-Gruppen bei Polizei", *Aachener Zeitung*, 16 September 2020; "Rechtsextremismus in der Polizei", *ZDF*, 6 October 2020

Page 64

"An entire underground network that was planning a coup...": Martin Kaul, Christina Schmidt, Daniel Schulz, "Hannibals Schattenarmee", *Taz*, 16 November 2018; Matthias Gebauer, Fidelius Schmid, Wolf Wiedmann-Schmidt "Franco A. wird nun doch angeklagt", *Der Spiegel*, 19 November 2019

BLOODY JEWS

Page 65

"The first recorded case of an accusation of ritual murder against a Jewish community": Miri Rubin, Thomas Monmouth, *The Life and Passion of William of Norwich*, London: Penguin, 2014 pviii. All references to narrative content refer to or quote from Miri Rubin's translation.

Page 66

"An open letter was posted on the online forum 8chan": full text of "John-T-Ernest-Manifesto-8chan-Pol-April-27-2019-An-Open-Letter", Internet Archive

"Thirteen Jews were executed": R Po-chia Hsia, *Trent 1475*, New Haven and London: Yale University Press, 1992, p127

"This did not have much effect in the long term": R Po-chia Hsia, *The Myth of Ritual Murder, Jews and Magic in Reformation Germany*, New Haven and London:Yale University Press,1988, p3

Page 67

"The 'ur-story' of English literary antisemitism": Anthony Julius, *Trials of the Diaspora*, Oxford: Oxford University Press, 2012, p153

Page 68

"The British fascist Arnold Leese": Arnold Leese, *My Irrelevant Defence: meditations inside gaol and out on Jewish ritual murder*, London: I.F.L. Printing & Pub., 1938, p39

"First arriving in England less than a hundred years previously with William the Conqueror": John M McCulloh, "Jewish Ritual Murder: William of Norwich, Thomas of Monmouth, and the Early Dissemination of the Myth", *Speculum*, July 1997, Vol 72, No 3, p737

Page 69

"This link between Jews past and Jews present had never before been so boldly attempted": Rubin, pxiv, pxxvii

"It is the Jewish people who insistently call for his crucifixion": Matthew 26:3-4; Luke 22:1-6; Luke 23: 13-24; Mark 14: 6-14; Matthew 27: 15-23

Page 70

"Thomas of Monmouth has been credited with inventing the ritual-murder charge": Gavin I Langmuir, "Thomas of Monmouth", in Alan Dundes (ed.), *The Blood Libel Legend: A Casebook in Anti-Semitic Folklore*, Madison: University of Wisconsin Press, 1991, p34

Page 71

"Single-page broadsheets": R Po-chia Hsia, pp46-50

"Vampires, whose bloodsucking diet and hooked nose recast the medieval fear of Jews in Gothic clothing": Carol Margaret Davison, *Anti-Semitism and British Gothic Literature*, Basingstoke and New York: Palgrave Macmillan, 2004, pp87-157

"The QAnon conspiracy theory": Mike McIntire and Kevin Roose, "What Happens When QAnon Seeps From the Web to the Offline World", *New York Times*, 9 February 2020

"Wrote the chronicler Matthew Paris": Matthew Paris's English History, Vol III, London: Henry G Bohn, 1854, p138-141

Page 72

"I am at a loss to understand why revivalist singers keep on singing it": Vic Gammon, sleeve notes, "Sir Hugh", *Brambles Briars and Beams of the Sun*, AL Lloyd, Fellside Recordings, 2011

"The American scholar Francis James Child": Francis James Child (ed.), *The English and Scottish Popular Ballads* Vol III, New York: Houghton Mifflin, 1957, p233-254

Page 73

"Newell paints a remarkable picture of extreme poverty": William Wells Newell, *Games and Songs of American Children*, New York, Harper and Brothers, 1884, pp75-78

"The British folk archivist Cecil Sharp": Cecil Sharp, *English Folk Songs from the Southern Appalachians*, London, Oxford University Press, 1960, pp222-229

Page 74

"Child cited a case in Tisza-Eszlar": Francis James Child, pp240-243

"Between 1867 and 1914, there were 12 ritual-murder trials [in Austria and German-Austria]": Peter Pulzer, *The Rise of Political Anti-Semitism in Germany and Austria*, Cambridge, MA: Harvard University Press, 1988, p69

Page 75

"In 1943, he wrote to the Reich's security chief": Dennis E Showalter, *Little Man, What Now? Der Stürmer in the Weimar Republic*, Hamden, CT: Shoe String Press, 1982, pp103-218

"The ritual murder charge was a 'tool' for extorting money": EM Rose, *The Murder of William of Norwich: The Origins of the Blood Libel in Medieval Europe*, Oxford, Oxford University Press, 2015, pp223, 235

"Leese described the publisher of Der Stürmer": Arnold Leese, p37

Page 76

"Colin Jordan ... was a follower": Daniel Trilling, *Bloody Nasty People*, London and New York: Verso, 2012, p54

"Antisemitic conspiracy theories remained central": Paul Jackson, "Conspiracy Theories and Neo-Nazism in the Cultic Milieu" in Asbjørn Dyrendal, David G Robertson and Egil Asprem (eds), *Handbook of Conspiracy Theory and Contemporary Religion*, Leiden and Boston: Brill, 2018, p470

"Everything in this little book rang true": ibid., p50

"The historian Ronnie Po-chia Hsia has credited the myth of child murders": R Po-chia Hsia, p208

Page 77

"American neo-Nazi Andrew Anglin posted an essay about ritual murder": Andrew Anglin, "Russia: Jew Woman Goes Nuts on the Bus, Threatens to Ritually Murder Goyim at the Synagogue", *Daily Stormer*, 16 April 2019

"He orchestrated online abuse of the British politician Luciana Berger": Andrew Anglin, "The Filthy Jew Bitch Luciana Berger Emerges from the Shadows to Attack Free Speech", *Daily Stormer*, 19 December 2014

"A US magistrate judge recommended that Anglin pay more than $14m in damages": Lois Beckett, "Judge advises $14m in damages to Jewish woman targeted by neo-Nazi 'troll storm'", *Guardian*, 16 July 2019

Page 79

"It is easy to spot the echoes of ritual murder in a cartoon": "Labour Councillor posts anti-Semitic propaganda", Order-order, 13 October 2016

"The local Labour group claimed that there was no evidence of similar previous conduct": "Anti-Semitism row: Councillor Andy Slack punished for 'insidious' Facebook post", *Derbyshire Times*, 25 October 2016

JEWS BEHAVING BADLY

Page 82

"If Jews continued to behave 'badly'": see Robert Fine and Philip Spencer, *Antisemitism and the Left: on the return of the Jewish Question*,

Manchester, Manchester University Press, 2017, pp16-18; Philip Spencer, "The shame of antisemitism on the left has a long, malign history", *Guardian*, 1 April 2018

"Some in the international communist movement argued": ibid. p49

Page 83

"This perception of Jews standing in the way of progress": see for example: Lee Harpin, "Jewish Question' speech given at Momentum 'Stand By Corbyn' rally", *Jewish Chronicle*, 1 November 2020

"They argued that antisemitism was being wilfully and dishonestly confused with anti-Zionism": this disingenuous argument has been most effectively discredited by David Hirsh in his *Contemporary Left Antisemitism*, Oxford and New York: Routledge, 2018

"The Equalities and Human Rights Commission (EHRC) opened an investigation": the full report may be found here: https://www.equality humanrights.com/en/publication-download/investigation-antisemitism-labour-party

Page 84

"Within western societies they have supposedly even become 'white'": Karen Brodkin, *How Jews Became White Folks and What That Says about Race in America*, New Brunswick, NJ: Rutgers University Press, 1998. A devastating critique of this whole way of thinking has been made by Balazs Berkovits in "Critical Whiteness Studies and the Jewish Problem", *Zeitschrift für kritische Sozialtheorie und Philosophie* 5, no. 1, 2018, pp 86–102

Page 85

"As the Pittsburgh massacre showed in 2018": "Pittsburgh shooting: who were the victims?", bbc.co.uk, 29 October 2018; "Synagogue massacre led to string of attack plots, Jewish group says", Associated Press, *Politico*, 20 October 2019

Page 86

"The 'anti-imperialism of fools'": for more on this, see Moishe Postone, "History and Helplessness: Mass Mobilization and Contemporary Forms of Anticapitalism," *Public Culture* 18, no. 1, 2006

Page 87

"The IHRA definition has been accepted by many governments": Lee Harpin, "Entire West Midlands region adopts IHRA definition of antisemitism", *Jewish Chronicle*, 1 September 2020

"The Labour Party tried to rewrite the Israel-related points": for a detailed critical analysis of this attempt, see "IHRA and the Labour Code of Conduct", Mark Gardner, Community Security Trust, 23 July 2018 https://cst.org.uk/news/blog/2018/07/11/what-is-the-international-holocaust-remembrance-alliance-definition-of-antisemitism

Page 88

"The figure of 33,771 Jews massacred at Babi Yar in Ukraine": Arno Lustiger, *Stalin and the Jews*, New York: Enigma, 2003, p106

"The manuscript and entire edition of The Black Book": "The Black Book of Soviet Jewry", Shoah Resource Center, Yad Vashem; Joshua Rubenstein and Vladimir P Naumov, *Stalin's Secret Pogrom: The Postwar Inquisition of the Jewish Anti-Fascist Committee*, New Haven: Yale University Press, 2001

Page 89

"Rename Holocaust Memorial Day as Genocide Memorial Day": Philip Spencer and Sara Valentina di Palma, "Antisemitism and the Politics of Holocaust Memorial Day in the UK and Italy", Gunther Jikeli and Joelle Allouche-Benayoun (eds), *Perceptions of the Holocaust in Europe and Muslim Communities*, Berlin: Springer, 2013

Page 91

"There has always been, however, another way of thinking on the left": for an

account of some of this history, and an analysis of the resources it offers for the left today, see, Robert Fine and Philip Spencer, op. cit. p.169

Page 92

"It is not wholly clear how much the problem of antisemitism played in this defeat": even if this were an important reason, however, it appears that after the defeat some 75 per cent of Labour Party members thought that antisemitism had been exaggerated in order to undermine Corbyn, even if half of them thought he should have done better to deal with the issue. The figure rose to 92 per cent for Momentum supporters. "Ninety-two percent of Momentum supporters think Labour antisemitism 'wildly exaggerated', poll shows", *Jewish Chronicle*, 11 February 2020

Page 93

"He was immediately suspended from the party": "Starmer: Anti-Semitism report 'day of shame' for Labour", bbc.co.uk, 29 October 2020; "Labour suspends Jeremy Corbyn over reaction to anti-Semitism report", bbc.co.uk, 30 October 2020

A LICENCE TO HATE

Page 94

"In 2019 the number of incidents hit an all-time high": Anti-Defamation League, "Antisemitic Incidents Hit All-Time High in 2019", 12 May 2020; Anti-Defamation League, A report from the Center on Extremism, "Murder and Extremism in the United States in 2019", February 2020

Page 95

"Wilhelm Marr...wrote in 1879": excerpted and translated in Richard S Levy, *The Victory of Jewry over Germandom*, DC Heath and Co, 1991

"Christian thinkers and leaders often conjured up a Jewish other": for a comprehensive and essential history of views about Jews in the Western World, see David Nirenberg, *Anti-Judaism: The Western Tradition*, New York: WW Norton, 2013

Page 97

"'Screw your optics, I'm going in'": Miriam Jordan, "HIAS, the Jewish Agency Criticized by the Shooting Suspect, Has a History of Aiding Refugees", *New York Times*, 28 October, 2018

Page 98

"As philosopher Karl Eugen Dühring wrote": Karl Eugen Dühring, "The Question of the Jew is a Question of Race", 1881

"One white supremacist Telegram channel": for more on the social media world of white supremacists, see Talia Lavin, *Culture Warlords: My Journey Into the Dark Web of White Supremacy*, New York: Hachette Books, 2020

"Anti-Semitism became a kind of 'cultural code'": David Sorkin, *Jewish Emancipation*, Princeton, NJ: Princeton University Press, 2019, p241

Page 99

"'200,000 Communist Jews at the Mexican border'": Josh Zeitz, "Yes, It's Fair to Compare the Plight of the Syrians to the Plight of the Jews. Here's Why", *Politico*, 22 November, 2015

"The Aryan Nations' 'Declaration of Independence'": https://archive.org/details/AryanNationsDeclaration

Page 101

"White supremacists were distributing antisemitic flyers": "Anti-Semitic Fliers Blaming Jews For Kavanaugh Allegations Found In Iowa", *Fast-Forward*, 11 October 2018

Page 102

"The majority of American Jews oppose settlement expansion": Ron Kampeas, "Most American Jews say you can support Israel and criticize its government", *Times of Israel*, 19 October 2018; Jeremy Sharon, "80% of US Jews say they are pro-Israel, study finds", *Jerusalem Post*, 4 February 2020

"A belief that Jews must all return to the Land of Israel": Richard Landes, "What Fuels Evangelical Christians' Love-hate Relationship With Jews", *Haaretz*, 29 July 2020

Page 103

"Even Trump acknowledged that his Israel policies cater to evangelicals": David Ian Klein, "Trump: Embassy move was for Evangelicals – Jews not excited about it", *Fast-Forward*, 18 August 2020

"The elevation of Christian pastors committed to supersessionist theology": Matthew Haag, "Robert Jeffress, Pastor Who Said Jews Are Going to Hell, Led Prayer at Jerusalem Embassy", *New York Times*, 14 May 2018

Page 104

"Trump's December 2019 Executive Order on Combating Antisemitism": "Executive Order on Combating Anti-Semitism", 11 December 2019, https://trumpwhitehouse.archives.gov/presidential-actions/executive-order-combating-anti-semitism/

"According to the International Holocaust Remembrance Alliance (IHRA) guidelines and examples": International Holocaust Remembrance Alliance, Working Definition of Antisemitism, https://www.holocaustremembrance.com/node/196

"Title VI 'provides protections to Jews, Arab Muslims, Sikhs, and/or members of other religious groups'": https://www.justice.gov/sites/default/files/crt/legacy/2011/05/04/090810_AAG_Perez_Letter_to_Ed_OCR_Title%20VI_and_Religiously_Identifiable_Groups.pdf

Page 106

"Criticism of Israel does sometimes cross the line into antisemitism": for a fuller exploration of when criticism of Israel crosses the line into antisemitism, see Rabbi Jill Jacobs, "How to Tell When Criticism of Israel is Actually Antisemitism," *Washington Post*, 17 May 2018

AFTERWORD

Page 126

"She said that she did not want to accept a new contract": Elizabeth A. Harris, "Sally Rooney Declines to Sell Translation Rights to Israeli Publisher," *New York Times*, 12 October 2021